CHICKEN SOUP FOR THE
WORKING MOM'S SOUL

CHICKEN SOUP
FOR THE
WORKING MOM'S
SOUL

Humor and Inspiration
for Moms Who Juggle It All

Jack Canfield
Mark Victor Hansen
Patty Aubery

Westland Ltd

We would like to acknowledge the following publishers and individuals for permission to reprint the following material.

When Mommy Is a Writer. Reprinted by permission of Sally Friedman. © 2007 Sally Friedman.

Mommy of the Board. Reprinted by permission of Pamela H. Hobson. © 2006 Pamela H. Hobson.

Pennies and Prayers. Reprinted by permission of Margaret L. Bert. © 2006 Margaret L. Bert.

A Privilege. Reprinted by permission of Harriet May Savitz. © 2005 Harriet May Savitz.

Modern Machines. Reprinted by permission of Felice R. Prager. © 2001 Felice R. Prager.

(Continued on page 299)

westland ltd
61, Silverline Building, Alapakkam Main Road, Maduravoyal, Chennai 600 095
No. 38/10 (New No.5), Raghava Nagar, New Timber Yard Layout, Bangalore 560 026
23/181, Anand Nagar, Nehru Road, Santacruz East, Mumbai 400 055
93, 1st Floor, Sham Lal Road, Daryaganj, New Delhi 110 002

This edition first published by Health Communications, Inc.
3201 S.W. 15th Street, Deerfield Beach, FL 33442-8190

First published in India by westland ltd 2008

This edition is for sale in India, Pakistan, Sri Lanka, Nepal and Bangladesh only

ISBN: 978-81-89975-94-4

Cover design by Larissa Hise Henoch
Inside formatting by Dawn Von Strolley Grove

Printed at Yash Printographics, Noida

Whether inside or outside the home, being a mom is a hard and challenging job.

This book is dedicated to all of you.

Contents

Acknowledgments xi

Introduction xiii

Share with Us xv

1. GOOD MOMS CAN WORK AND STILL HAVE GREAT KIDS

When Mommy Is a Writer *Sally Friedman* 2

Mommy of the Board *Pamela Hackett Hobson* 5

Pennies and Prayers *Peggy Bert* 7

A Privilege *Harriet May Savitz* 11

Modern Machines *Felice Prager* 14

The Best of Both Worlds *Mimi Greenwood Knight* 17

Boardroom Babies *Nicole M. Whitney* 20

From a Distance *Sheryl McCormick* 26

Framed *Joan Paquette* 29

Mother: Guilty as Charged *Stephanie Ray Brown* 32

2. "MOMMY" ON MY RESUME

The Playground Lady *Winter D. Prosapio* 36

A Working Mom's Retirement Plan *Linda O'Connell* 39

Learning to Smell the Roses *Tiffany O'Neill* 44

A Mom First *Kimberly Kimmel* 48

Happy Mother's Day *Ann Morrow* 52

Weaving a Web of Wise Words at Work *Tanya Tyler* 56

3. TAKING TIME FOR ME

Jumping In with Both Feet *Dahlynn McKowen* 61

Chat and Chew *Pamela Hackett Hobson* 64

Making Memories *Jo Webnar* 67

My Day Off *Judy Spence* 72

A Home of My Own *Elizabeth Bussey Sowdal* 75

Earning the Privilege of Being Sick *Mary Vallo* 78

The Contract *Stephanie Welcher Thompson* 81

4. ENLISTING EXTRA HELP!

The Choice *Stephanie Chandler* 86

Another Calling *Mimi Greenwood Knight* 90

The Button *Vanessa Ann Cain* 94

That Ugly Thing *Maryjo Faith Morgan* 98

Dear Working Mom *Mindy Potts* 100

You Are So Special to Me *Christina Guzman* 102

Are They Your Stepchildren? *Jennifer Oliver* 104

A Mom for Working Moms *Eva Juliuson* 108

Angels in Seminole *Stephen A. Peterson* 112

Being a Working Mom *Dorothy Megan Clifton* 116

Waving the White Flag *Deborah Shouse* 118

To Toast a Dad *Jo Ann Holbrook* 121

Relearning How to Say Good-bye *Maya Fleischmann* 125

A Simple Recipe *Linda Hanson* 128

Mom-entum *Jennifer Nicholson* 132

5. SUPERWOMAN—JUGGLING IT ALL

The Breast Pump *Ken Swarner* 137

Interview *Elizabeth Bussey Sowdal* 140

The Ideal Situation *Melanie Howard* 143

In Mom We Trust *Diane M. Covington* 147

Notes Left by Two Working Parents *Ken Swarner* 152

There's No Such Thing as a Part-Time Mom *Karen Cogan* 156

The Best of Both Worlds *Debi Callies* 159

The Glamorous Life as a Novelist *Erica Orloff* 162

Of Mice, Men, and the *New York Times* *Sally Friedman* 166

Morning Glory *Elizabeth Bussey Sowdal* 171

6. THROUGH THE EYES OF A CHILD

A Child's Playground *Tony Gilbert* 176

We're Out of Food *Pamela Teague* 181

The Value of Money *Lynda Johnson* 183

Out of the Mouths of Babes *Miriam Hill* 187

Too Much Work *Cynthia Morningstar* 188

What's in It for Us Is Good *Arlene Uslander* 189

Hi Ho, Hi Ho, It's Off to Work I Go—Not *Crystal Davis* 192

7. A MATTER OF PERSPECTIVE

Eight Days a Week *Pamela Hackett Hobson* 196

Shortcuts and Illusions *Jane Elsdon* 198

Dog Days *Elizabeth Bussey Sowdal* 201

Learning to Fly *Britt Prince* 204

Hugs and Kisses *Susan Courtad* 208

The New Age To-Do List *Shirley Warren* 212

Balancing *Margaret P. Cunningham* 216

The Little Computer That Wouldn't *Carol Mell* 220
Real Summers *Mary Dixon Lebeau* 224

8. INSIGHTS AND LESSONS

A Lesson Learned When Tying Shoelaces *Margaret Haefner Berg* 228
Are You Listening? *Jennifer L. White* 231
Little Sounds *Peggy Frezon* 235
Mustaches on Cherubs *Margaret Lang* 238
Every Day Is a Good Day *Kathleen Partak* 241
Moms Know Everything *Emily Rider-Longmaid* 244
Sick Day *Brenda Rosales Rincon* 246
Paving the Road from Nanna to Mamma *Pat Moore* 250
Prioritize to Simplify Your Life *Sharon McElroy* 254
The Road to Independence *Pat Winters Lauro* 257
Dandelions and My Little Samantha *Dorothy K. Fletcher* 261
Fate and Hindsight *Jan Morrill* 265
Back in the Saddle Again *Bernetta Thorne-Williams* 269
Beware the "I'ds" of March *Heather Cook* 273
Engraved on the Pages of Life *Betty King* 275
Storm Day *Bonnie Jarvis-Lowe* 279

More Chicken Soup? 283
Supporting Others 284
Who Is Jack Canfield? 286
Who Is Mark Victor Hansen? 287
Who Is Patty Aubery? 288
Contributors 289
Permissions *(continued)* 299

Acknowledgments

We wish to express our heartfelt gratitude to all of the people who helped make this book possible:

Our families, who have been chicken soup for our souls by supporting us as we continue to serve our readers endlessly!

Our publisher and friend, Peter Vegso, for his continuous support and allegiance to all of us and to the Chicken Soup brand.

Russ Kalmaski, the most amazing chief operating officer on the planet, who can take any situation and make it simple.

D'ette Corona, our coauthor liaison, who seamlessly manages twenty to thirty projects at a time. Without D'ette, none of these projects would happen.

Patty Hansen, our president of the legal and licensing division. Patty is magnificent at the day-to-day challenges.

Veronica Romero, Barbara Lomonaco, Teresa Collette, Robin Yerian, Jesse Ianniello, and Lauren Edelstein, all of whom continue to support our Santa Barbara operation with joy and enthusiasm.

Lisa Williams, thank you for your endless hours of time helping us to find just the right cover image.

Laurie Hartman and Patti Clement, who support our

Costa Mesa operation with skill and love.

Michele Matrisciani, Carol Rosenberg, Andrea Gold, Allison Janse, and Katheline St. Fort, our editors at Health Communications, Inc., for their devotion to excellence.

Terry Burke, Lori Golden, Kelly Maragni, Sean Geary, Patricia McConnell, Ariana Daner, Kim Weiss, Paola Fernandez-Rana, for doing such an incredible job supporting our books.

Tom Sand, Claude Choquette, and Luc Jutras, who manage year after year to get our books translated into more than forty languages around the world.

Larissa Hise Henoch and Andrea Perrine Brower for their talent, creativity, and unrelenting patience while producing book covers and inside designs that capture the essence of Chicken Soup.

Ken and Dahlynn McKowen, for editing the final manuscript with such enthusiasm. Your willingness to help and your friendship mean the world to all of us.

Thank you to Stephanie Chandler for your chapter ideas; we really appreciate all your help and enthusiasm.

And, most of all, thanks to everyone who submitted their heartfelt stories, poems, quotes, and cartoons for possible inclusion in this book. While we were not able to use everything you sent in, we know that each word came from a magical place flourishing within your soul.

Because of the size of this project, we may have left out the names of some people who contributed along the way. If so, we are sorry, but please know that we really do appreciate you very much. We are truly grateful and love you all!

Introduction

"Working mom" is redundant. All moms are working moms! And that is exactly what this book is about, to honor all moms, from those who stay at home to those who work outside the home, and even those who fit in between.

In creating this title, we had a difficult time deciding which stories to publish because each and every one was so varied in its definition of a "working mom." While many of the stories made us smile, many more touched our souls and opened our hearts to just how hard it is to raise a family while working. This is evident in the chapter entitled "Taking Time for Me": we received very few story submissions for this chapter, which proved to us that working moms rarely get time for themselves!

We invite you to enjoy the stories found within and apply your personal definition of your life as a working mom. And luckily, you can savor the book one story at a time, as we know moms are the busiest women in the world!

Share with Us

We would love to hear your reactions to the stories in this book. Please let us know what your favorite stories were and how they affected you.

We also invite you to send us stories you would like to see published in future editions of Chicken Soup for the Soul. Please send submissions to www.chickensoup.com.

Chicken Soup for the Soul
P.O. Box 30880
Santa Barbara, CA 93130
Fax: 805-563-2945

We hope you enjoy reading this book as much as we enjoyed compiling, editing, and writing it.

1

GOOD MOMS CAN WORK AND STILL HAVE GREAT KIDS

People take different roads seeking fulfillment and happiness. Just because they are not on your road doesn't mean they've gotten lost.

H. Jackson Brown, Jr.

When Mommy Is a Writer

"And what do you do?" the gentleman seated to my right at a dinner party politely asked me. I was about thirty-two years old and the mother of three little girls.

"I'm a mom," I answered proudly.

"Oh, so you don't work?" He sniffed.

I will never forget the way this well-pedigreed captain of industry turned away from me in an instant to pursue a conversation with the woman on his other side—hopefully, somebody with a life.

And I never forgot the sympathetic looks, the rude withdrawals, the assumption that I was surely not important enough or enlightened enough to make decent conversation.

The women who were just starting to emerge in careers of their own back in the changing 1970s were sometimes equally disdainful. It was the era when all things seemed possible for women; Betty Friedan's book *The Feminine Mystique* announced that the world was bigger than a baked potato. And suddenly, work was the answer to getting beyond the kitchen walls.

I was one of those women who didn't work "outside the home," as we were careful to enunciate, until my three daughters were safely launched in school at least for most of the day. I loved those years at home. But to be perfectly frank, I also found myself occasionally wondering whether I'd ever get my turn to do what I wanted.

It came. But in a carefully selected way.

I became a mommy-writer. In what turned out to be a perfect synthesis for me, I wrote about being a mom. That writing turned into a column. That column turned into something of a local institution that still goes on, thirty-three years and counting. My daughters grew up in my column, which made life both interesting and challenging for them—and for me.

Where were the boundaries? Was it fair to share with thousands of readers how Jill fared on her first date? How it felt when Amy and I, the glorious battlers in our family, stormed in and out of each other's lives? When Nancy, the "baby," left for college, and I had to leave the door of her room closed for months rather than weep each time I saw it empty?

Because my working life and home life collided constantly, it was sometimes impossible to figure out where one began and the other ended. My daughters were my "material." And to make matters more complicated, they could all read by the time I started writing for a living. Never mind that my husband, a judge with a very public life, would have welcomed some privacy.

So in hindsight, would I have done anything—or everything—differently? Did my mommy life and my career have to be so inextricably intertwined? And so consuming?

Yes. No. Maybe . . .

Working from a home office, surrounded by laundry baskets, entertained by cries of "She hit me first!" and "I hate her!" and constantly battling the push-pull of *Do I beg for an extension on my deadline so that I can go with the Brownie troop to the petting zoo?* defined my life for years. Decades.

Like so many working mothers, I seemed in a constant

war with myself. And the very nature of my work—revelation—meant that I often spilled the beans on my family to my readers.

All these years later, my daughters tell me that despite their furies, despite the times they slammed their doors in my face as if to say, "This will keep you out of my life," they kind of liked their celebrity. Now they tell me that it was "cool" to have a mom who made them, well, kind of famous in the local sense.

What makes all of this seem to have yet another life is that now I'm writing about their children, our seven brilliant, beautiful, and altogether stupendous grandchildren!

"Grandma, stop writing about me!" the "larges," as we call the older children of the bunch, lament. But I've been this route before, and I strongly suspect that Hannah, Isaiah, Sam, and Jonah don't really mean it. I've even overheard them boasting to their schoolyard buddies, "My name was in the paper again!"

The "smalls," Danny, Emily, and Carly, can't read yet. I count it as a blessing, for now.

So will I go on doing this? Will I shamelessly make my life as a wife, mother, grandmother, woman—and my career—a complicated fusion?

I'm afraid so.

Because "living out loud" as the wonderful writer Anna Quindlen calls it, can become gloriously, hopelessly addictive.

Sally Friedman

Mommy of the Board

The best effect of fine persons is felt after we have left their presence.

Ralph Waldo Emerson

Although I loved my job at a top Wall Street bank, I jumped at the chance to work for a financial services company located much closer to my home. With a young son just starting kindergarten, a chance to reduce my two and one-half hour daily commute and have more time with my family was an opportunity that was too good to pass up.

My new employer was embarking on a period of tremendous growth and expansion. The employees, the chairman of the bank, and the newly elected board members were energized by the possibilities. I was pleased to learn that one of the founding members of *Ms. Magazine* had recently joined the executive board to help steer the organization in the right direction. Senior management was anxious to demonstrate to their newest board member that their commitment to hire and promote qualified women was more than just words. Although only a junior officer, I was asked to be the first woman to make a presentation to the board to explain many of the new programs and policies we had recently introduced. Suppressing a gulp, I accepted the challenge.

The morning of the presentation was a typical day in my incredibly busy household. I woke early to shower and dress, put on makeup, throw in a load of laundry, take the meat out to defrost for dinner, study my note cards, wake my son, get him dressed and fed, check his backpack, remember to sign yet another permission slip, check the family calendar to see what the after-school activity or playdate arrangement was for the day, drop my son off at school, rush to the train and spend a few quality minutes alone with my husband (read: remind each other about the need to schedule doctor/dentist/school appointments), and speed walk from Grand Central Station to the executive offices just off Park Avenue.

Entering the executive suite, the president of the bank greeted me and asked if I was ready to meet with the board. I assured him that I was definitely all set and followed his instructions to wait outside the boardroom until called. Senior management was almost as nervous as I because no one at my level had ever made a presentation to the board before. A lot was riding on this meeting, and we all wanted it to come off without a hitch.

Just minutes before I entered the room, I performed a last minute check to be sure my corporate gray suit was presentable. Smoothing my jacket pocket, I found what was disrupting the clean line of my designer suit. Reaching inside the pocket, I found the culprit and smiled. My son's favorite miniature car was idling in my pocket, just waiting for the moment when I would pick him up later that day. I carefully placed the car back inside my suit pocket, opened the door to the boardroom, and with my son's presence firmly by my side, drove his car full speed ahead.

Pamela Hackett Hobson

Pennies and Prayers

The three of us were gathered around our breakfast table. My husband, Alex, swallowed the last few drops of his coffee, pushed his chair away from the table, and kissed us good-bye.

It was 7:00 AM on a Monday morning.

Our three-year-old son was perched on his booster chair, wearing cowboy pajamas, bunny-rabbit slippers, and a corduroy robe. He looked up at us intently through oversized, sparkling blue eyes with long, fluttering lashes. Chewing his Cheerios, he started asking his usual questions.

"Is today a go-to-work day?"

"Yes, sweetheart, it is."

"Can I go, too?"

"No, honey."

"Does Daddy have to go to work?"

"Yes, he does."

"Why does Daddy have to go to work?"

"Daddy has to go to work to make money. We need money to live in this apartment and buy food and milk and juice and cereal at the grocery store. We need money to buy other things, like our television, these dishes, and hamburgers and ice cream at McDonald's. We need money for all that. If Daddy doesn't go to work, we won't have any money."

This Monday morning was going to be very different from all the others. Today, I, too, was leaving for work. Alex had just changed careers, and his compensation was now based solely on the promise of future commissions. We decided that I would begin working outside the home to help supplement our income until he got established. New questions from our son were sure to follow.

"But why do you have to go to work, Mommy?"

"Well, Vince, Mommy is going to work because we need just a little extra money."

All of sudden, those big blue eyes of his lit up, as if he actually understood what we were trying to tell him. He jumped from his chair and took off running down the hall for his bedroom. We heard him open a drawer of his dresser, and then a "clinking" sound filled the air. The *clink-clink-clink* kept getting louder. It matched the cadence of running feet. Vince appeared, clutching his piggy bank to his chest.

Each time grammas, grandpas, aunts and uncles, or friends came over, they gave Vince money. He gripped every coin with his elfin fingers and carefully positioned each one to drop through the narrow slot. One at a time they clinked into his chubby yellow plastic pig. We thought this was a valuable tool to teach our son the concept of saving money. We explained to him that after there were many coins inside, he could use them for something very special. He counted the contents often and always referred to it as "my money."

He proudly raised his plump little piggy toward us. Still panting, with excitement in his voice and a big smile on his face, he said, "I'll give you all my money so you can stay home, and we can all be together."

We couldn't speak. The lumps in our throats brought tears to our eyes. A sharp, cruel arrow of guilt penetrated deep into my spirit. Could it ever be successfully removed? It felt like my heart had been wounded beyond repair. Could I ever forget the words my child just spoke? Would that look of anticipation in his eyes ever leave the camera of my mind? Had we made a mistake? Was the decision we made for me to work outside the home a bad one? Our desire was only to do what we thought best for our family.

That incident took place thirty-two years ago. In the years since, we have learned how to seek God's guidance in our decisions and our finances. If at times we felt we had made a mistake, we entrusted the outcome to God in faith.

That blue-eyed "boy" now flies 757 and 767 jet aircraft all over the world as captain for a major airline. Because of his profession, he lives in a different state than we do. Just recently, we enjoyed a memorable seven-day visit at our son's home. A major topic of conversation during our stay was the possibility of our buying a condo as a second home in the area where he lives.

The three of us were sitting around his breakfast table. Sipping his coffee, Vince looked up at us with his sparkling eyes and said, "Listen, Mom and Dad, don't worry about the money part of it. I've saved a lot over the years, and I can pay your taxes and fees and whatever expenses you need help with. Just do it, and we can all be together in the same place."

Some things never change—piggy banks are profitable partners. We have contacted a real estate agent and will fly back to look at property. God's protective, loving hand can help overcome obstacles and mend a mother's heart; it is filled with overflowing gratitude, not guilt.

Peggy Bert

A Privilege

I was a working mother, and now I am a working grand-mother. As a writer, I work at home. I make my own hours, do not have to worry about wardrobe or transportation, and often look as if I am not working at all. Other working mothers and grandmothers who leave each morning for their jobs often look my way and say, "You're so lucky, not having to work."

Of course I am working. Because I can withstand any-thing, cope with anything, I can deal with the surprises and catastrophes of life as long as I have my work. My spot. My moment of expression. I felt that I would be a better mother then, and I feel I'm a better grandmother today if I have something that is just mine. All mine. Whether it be for fame or for fortune. Or just for the love of it. Work.

My children grew up eating their lunches on my manuscripts, sitting on my desk to talk with me, and thinking that all mothers slept with a notebook and pen beside their beds. My husband knew the greatest gift he could give me was a typewriter and time staring out a window where an idea might be lurking. I was not the kind of mother who attended all the school events, or who cooked memorable meals. I did not sew, bake, or clean house to anyone's delight—and still do not. But I can write. That is my work, where I feel special. Where my identity has a voice.

It has always been this way. I need to get housework done so that I can work. I need to get that meal on the table so that I can work. Work became the bonus. The prize. The gift I received so that I might give more back to others. More of my satisfied self. More of the self still in the works.

There were sacrifices. I was not "super mom." Sometimes I was too tired to enjoy special moments. Sometimes I was frustrated and angry with myself and could not offer my children all they might have wanted. Sometimes, I guess, I did not measure up, or possibly I let them down. But there were precious moments that survived the years. The peanut butter and jelly crackers in stacks waiting for them at the end of the school day. The bedtime stories when I jumped into bed with them. The intimate conversations that would survive a lifetime. No work could steal those times from me. My job did not leave me because it was the end of a day or arrive because it was the beginning. It remained, day and night, as my comfort, as my inspiration, and sometimes as my tormentor. When my husband watched me trying to cope after my cancer operation, he said, "Go work. You'll feel better." And I did.

My children watched me work in my underwear, in my bed, in sickness, and in despair. "What are you doing?" they asked in the middle of the night when they found me sitting at my desk.

"Working," was my reply. For I feel work is a privilege. Sometimes it expects everything. And sometimes it gives everything.

I never made a living as a freelance writer. Writers seldom do. It wasn't my income that kept me working. And it wasn't the people I worked with, for there were none.

And it wasn't the praise that I received, because there was more rejection than praise. I kept working because work broadened my world and my perception of it.

Now in my seventies, I have more time than I did when the children were young. More hours in the day that are free. I could relax. Retire. Take it easy. Or learn how to cook a memorable meal. I could, but I won't. For those who might think me old or finished, I answer, "Not yet. I am still working."

Harriet May Savitz

Modern Machines

I received three e-mails from my mother today. This is unusual because until today, my mother didn't own a computer. She's watched me work on my assorted computers, which occupy my office and my kids' bedrooms. For us, computers are a way of life. We are the modern twenty-first century family.

The first e-mail from my mother said: *Believe it or not—I'm on the line. It took a long time. Call you later. Mom.*

I figured by "on *the* line" she meant "online" and laughed at her interpretation.

The second e-mail said: *I'm just learning, don1t mind the mistakes. I bought a Dell like you suggested. Eventually I!ll know what I!m doing. gIVE mE A lITTLE tIME. Love you Mom.* This was all written in the subject line of the e-mail. The body was empty.

I didn't want to burst my mother's bubble and tell her that she might never know what she's doing on a computer. So I sent her a reply explaining that the apostrophe and quotation marks are no longer over the 1 and 8 like they used to be on her old Smith Corona manual typewriter. I explained where they were on a computer keyboard. It had taken my mom so long to overcome her fear of computers and actually buy one that I wanted to help ease her anxiety by keeping it simple. I explained in my reply how to write an e-mail and how to save interesting websites she might want to revisit. I sent her links to some of my favorite places and some of the work I've had published online. Then I wrote, "Just have fun with this new cyber world. Don't worry about breaking anything or doing something wrong. You can't break the Internet or your computer by clicking the wrong box. And if you mess something up, I can fix it for you!"

When I was in elementary school, my mother was one of the few moms who worked outside the home. In the late fifties and early sixties, other mothers stayed home with the kids; mine worked because she had no other choice. Some mothers made cookies. My mother typed my reports for me on crisp office paper, with carbon copies. In my case, the situation was ideal. The office where my mother worked was across the street from my school. She was often able to coordinate her lunch hour with mine, and I was none the worse for it. We'd visit a local coffee shop and eat grilled cheese sandwiches together. I'd have a chocolate egg cream; she'd have black coffee, no sugar.

I remember when I took typing in high school, a required course for all students going to college or secretarial school, and I finally made it to typing forty words per minute; my mother was typing sixty-five words or more. I tested her once for fun at eighty words per minute and no errors. She didn't even break a sweat. She was an incredible typist. In those days, fixing errors required specialized typewriter erasers that tended to rip the paper if pressed too hard against the print; however, my mother was the master of her trade. She typed fast and rarely made an error that she couldn't fix with ease.

The third e-mail my mother sent was a reply to the e-mail I had sent. It was also written all in the subject line, nothing in the body of the e-mail: *Why did they move the apostrophe and quotes? There was nothing wrong with where they were. I'm going to write Dell a letter about it. Love Mom.*

Today my mother took a big step. She is on the road to being computer literate. With as much tact as I could muster, I told my mother today where to find the apostrophe and the quotation marks, and she told me, in an e-mail, what I could do with them.

Felice Prager

The Best of Both Worlds

"I work at home for my children's sake!" I repeat this to myself until maybe I can believe it. Too often lately I feel like the worst parent on the planet. As a freelance writer, I make my own hours and can work at home with my kids. A good deal, right? Not always.

Some days I take four-year-old Hewson to the park. The older kids are at school, I'm staring at a deadline, but I'm eaten up with guilt because I'm not spending time with him. Then I think, *Hey, I'm my own boss! We can go to the park! I can work while he plays—the best of both worlds.* I grab my cell phone and my laptop, and pull into the park, thinking, *Yes! You can have it all!*

The next thing I know, I'm sitting on a park bench with my laptop balanced on my knees while in front of me three mommies push their preschoolers on swings, alternately giving my son a push and giving me that we-all-make-choices-we-have-to-live-with look. Or maybe I'm imagining it.

Then other days, like today, when I absolutely, positively, no-questions-asked have to get some writing done, three little people who just want their mama are on the other side of my office door. Seven-year-old Molly slips into the room. "Mom, will you get the water colors down for me?"

I close my eyes and pray for patience. I know I could stop working and get the paints down for her. It would take half a minute. But I also know that as soon as I set foot out of this room, I'll hear "We want some ice cream!" "When can we go to the library?" "You said we'd go for a walk!" "When are you going to stop working, Mama?"

I take my hands off the keyboard, swivel my chair in her direction, take a deep breath, and begin the conversation I have had at least a dozen times a week. "Honey, what is Mommy's job?" I've asked this question so many times that each of my children has a memorized answer.

Haley at age nine understands. "You're a writer, Mom."

Hewson at age four usually manages something like, "You work on the computer," which he pronounces *bu-cud-a.*

Molly gets that here-we-go-again look and concedes. "You write stories."

"That's right. And where do I write stories?"

She groans. "At home so you can be with us."

I launch into my treatise on how lots of mommies have to work away from their children, how it would break my heart to do that, how we're lucky I can work at home and spend more time with them that way, but how, right now, I must work because this is something I have to finish today!

Now, in theory, Molly has no problem with letting me get my work done. But to children everything is immediate and right now, and right this second, Molly wants the water colors, and I realize this conversation is like verbal chewing gum. I can sit here chomping on it all day, and when I'm through she'll want to know, "So, when are you getting the water colors, Mom?"

I get up, walk into the den, get the paints, and try a new tactic. "Okay, guys, now that I'm up, does anybody need anything else?" Silence. I stop and give each child a kiss, a hug, and tell them I love them. Then I announce that I'm getting into my car. I pantomime getting into an invisible car and make a sound like I'm starting it up. They stare at me slack-jawed. "Now I'm driving to my office." I drive myself across the den, climb out of my imaginary car. "Now I'm at my office. I'm going to work, and I'll see you all in one hour." I step into the office and close the doors behind me. (Glass office doors may be part of my problem. If out of sight is out of mind, the opposite is certainly true.)

I slump back in my computer chair, stare at the words on the screen, and try to remember what in the world I was writing. This is hard! I tell myself it's better than working away from them. I answer myself that it may be better but it certainly isn't easier.

I brave a look through the office doors. Molly is hard at work on her painting, content for the time being. Haley and Hewson are on the couch, reading a book. They're really great kids. I wasn't kidding when I said it would break my heart to be away from them. In a little while, when I'm finished working, they'll be on the other side of those doors waiting for me. There's no time wasted commuting back to them, no office politics to work around. I've got the flexibility to be here when they need me, enough money to do the things we want to do when I'm not tied to the computer, the chance to scratch my creative itch, an extremely relaxed dress code, and all the peanut butter and gummi bears I care to eat. Now that I think about it, maybe this is the best of both worlds.

The door opens and there's Haley. "Hey, Mom, when are we going to the library?"

Sigh.

Mimi Greenwood Knight

Boardroom Babies

Nothing happens unless first a dream.

Carl Sandburg

It was the late 1990s, and my life held little promise. Truthfully, I spent most hours in fear. I had two children, three incurable diseases, and I was alone. My life pretty much started out in darkness and stayed on that course.

I was given up at birth and never saw a blood relative until I gave birth to one. If I had to say something positive about my life while growing up, I'd say two things: one, I made it, and two, it created who and what I am today.

When I was in my early thirties, I was officially "rubber stamped" by the British Columbia government in Canada as permanently disabled. The reality of that "achievement" permeated my consciousness and left little room for future promise or passion for myself or for the two children I was raising alone.

At that time I was experiencing three incurable diseases. The most serious was Crohns disease, an inflammatory bowel situation that's best not discussed at the dinner table or during business meetings. I also had iritis and associative arthritis that left me intermittently blind, in pain, and periodically walking with a cane.

At one point I was working part-time as a freelance journalist, the only kind of work I was able to juggle around sickness, children, and my desolate no-light-at-the-end-of-the-tunnel reality.

During the winter of 1997, a strange thought "popped" into my head. I decided that rather than work with the mainstream news media, I would start my own "positive news" newspaper. For someone immersed in negativity, disempowerment, limitations, and struggle, this was a random and obscure line of thinking, indeed. But the thought would not go away. In fact, I tried to make it go away. You see, I had no family, resources, or support system. Moreover, I certainly had no knowledge or experience—practical, theoretical, or otherwise—about publishing a newspaper. I did have plenty of excellent reasons why *not* to do this. The thought of making a contribution to both the world and my family's way of life, security, and future helped outweigh the enormous list of cons—and so my adventure began.

After a couple months of planning and solo thought incubation that bordered on obsession, my first little positive-news newspaper hit Vancouver streets in January 1998! It was a small, odd-looking paper and contained only two ads. It was a wonderful family achievement from start to finish.

In the early months I manually "pasted-up" the newspaper on my living room floor using old-fashioned blue line flats, spending hours painstakingly aligning ads and columns of text in my twenty-four-page paper. My one-year-old, Brieonda, often "helped" by unpasting headlines off the flats and onto her forehead or derriere, proudly crawling around the living room to display her handiwork for all to see.

I appointed eight-year-old Christina as the kids' columnist and sent her into the community on assignment. She covered everything from Adventure Kids Camp experiences to movies and entertainment. For her restaurant reviews, she sampled everything from fine dining to fries and "wrote it up" for each edition. A few months into our newspaper project, Christina interviewed her first "dignitary," the mayor of Coquitlam in British Columbia. I'm not sure which of them was more terrified. It was all I could do not to burst into laughter as I watched the nervous pair turn similar shades of scarlet during the twenty-minute tête-à-tête. She also once covered a comedic Shakespeare performance. In her story she referred to the man who led the troupe as "the throwee up guy." A framed copy of her review still hangs on his office wall today.

Our little family was all too familiar with the dreaded distribution department. Newspaper delivery took place every month around the time we'd just recovered from the previous month's job. Delivering ten thousand of anything in your spare time is no easy task.

When I wasn't writing, designing, or delivering papers, I sold advertising. I dropped into local businesses doing "cold call" advertising sales, a task I didn't enjoy. But this was part of the job, and I had kids to feed and dreams to reach. I'd arrive, wild-haired, flushed, and sweaty, propping the door open with one foot as I pushed through my load: the baby, the buggy, an overstuffed baby bag, a briefcase weighted down with newspapers, plus my purse with the cell phone buried at the very bottom of the heap. As you can probably imagine, our appearance generated a wide range of reactions.

Some of my potential clients eagerly interacted with my "little person" for a few moments. It presented a welcome diversion and an excuse to be silly. Working moms openly welcomed us. They demonstrated an understanding of

my challenges by providing cracker snacks or office supplies for a mini craft-making session while we "did business." Others would take a man-all-battle-stations stance
as we entered the foyer, battening down any potential
breakables, never taking their eyes off my child. These
meetings often were particularly short.

One memorable appointment was with the president of
a large, family restaurant chain. After a phone tag game
that should have qualified us for an Olympic medal, I
finally pinned down a meeting time. I had actually booked
a sitter for this meeting, but at the last moment she canceled. Thus, I arrived at my meeting as gracefully as ever
and was led, baby buggy and all, into a tiny but comfy private meeting room. I waited apprehensively for the company president to enter.

I figured, hey, it's only twenty minutes. We could get
through it.

Just then, the company president entered the room.
With a brief but discernable sideways glance at my "associate," he dispensed a friendly greeting. After a few
moments of "weather chitchat," our meeting began—and
so did my daughter. I had come fully prepared with
crayons, toys, and favorite treats. Unfortunately, her 2:00 PM
nap time was fast approaching; for toddlers, that's a time
akin to a vampire eyeing the approach of the rising sun.

At first, my second born simply emitted a few strategi-
cally timed mutters and grunts. By the five-minute mark
she reached full-fledged whines. I forged ahead with my
sales presentation while handing my increasingly loud
toddler an endless stream of potentially amusing items
and snacks, shaking them maniacally in front of her. To my
horror, she displayed complete disinterest in everything.

She soon launched full-scale war, picking up the box of
Smarties that I'd hoped would capture her interest. She
carefully opened it, changed the whines to full-on yells,

and opened fire, launching a rainbow of tiny candy missiles, one at a time, right at my potential client's head.

"So, tell me about your demographics," the company's president asked. It was just then that a particularly well-thrown red Smartie nailed the man right on the nose, making an eerie *BLAPP* that echoed for several seconds in the now silent conference room.

My jaw dropped, my daughter stopped—completely—and the man who would have been my next advertising customer peered down at the offending object for a moment and then looked at my daughter who was still staring at his nose.

After what seemed an eternity, he picked up the red candy assault weapon and—ate it!

"Mmmm. The red ones are my favorite," he said, smiling.

My daughter giggled.

I left with a full-page ad and the knowledge that, single mom or not, anything was possible!

Nicole M. Whitney

"My kids will be interning here, until
something opens up in child care!"

From a Distance

In 2003, as a single parent of a sweet little four-year-old boy named Dylan and as a soldier in the Canadian military, I was going on deployment to the Middle East, although to a location that was considered safe. Having been recently divorced and dealing with the challenges of a shared custody agreement and being a completely devoted parent, I knew this would not be an easy thing to do. I truly believed I was helping our son by giving his dad a chance to be with him without me around, so he could focus on Dylan and provide a stable home for him, emotionally and physically.

I left home on December 31, 2003. I had been told we'd be gone anywhere from six to nine months to an undisclosed location in the Middle East. I had packed several self-addressed stamped envelopes with a blank piece of paper in each into Dylan's backpack so that he could draw pictures and mail them to me. One of my most vivid memories in my life was when I dropped Dylan off at his dad's house. I will always remember Dylan standing on the couch in the living room window, waving at me and blowing kisses with tears streaming down his face as I drove away. I don't know how I could see him or the road through my tears. I felt like my heart was being ripped out of my chest.

Once I was on the plane, I had a slight sense of relief because the decision was made and there was no turning back. At the same time and for the same reason, I had a sense of panic. I was already looking forward to receiving drawings from my wonderful little boy.

The first thing I did when we arrived was to look for a phone, so I could call Dylan. The camp was well set up with several phone booths. Hearing Dylan's voice through the phone lines made the distance seem less; still my heart literally ached. I wanted to reach out and hug him, but I knew it would be a long time until I could.

Even with my busy schedule and many work challenges, my mind never drifted far from thoughts of Dylan. We didn't live far from civilization, so I was able to buy cards, postcards, toys, clothes, and candy and send packages to Dylan, so he knew I was thinking of him. Prior to leaving, I taped Dylan "reading" along with his read-along stories. At my lowest times, especially when I had tried unsuccessfully day after day to talk with him on the phone, I would bring out my tape recorder and listen to his voice. Hearing him would bring sadness to my heart, but at the same time I felt a sense of pride for the great little person that he is and it made me feel closer to him. I had also videotaped us reading together and told him to ask his dad to play it for him when he was missing me.

On one of my trips into civilization, we came across a store where you could build your own teddy bear. I jumped at this and recorded my voice saying how much I missed him and loved him, and they sewed it up with a heart inside blessed with my kisses. I could hear his excitement through the phone lines when he received the bear.

I would get up at night to call because the time difference was ten hours. I also called the day care to find out how he was doing there. This was an arrangement I made before I left to ensure Dylan's well-being because my conversations with his dad were limited. They reported he was doing well and sent me updates. To Dylan's dad's credit, he did send several pictures that Dylan had drawn. Between the drawings and the photos I brought with me, my room was decorated in "Dylan wallpaper." His face was the first I'd see when I woke up and the last I'd see before I fell asleep. I kept pictures of him at work as well, so I was never without him.

I was relieved to find out that we had an end date of six months, which was so much better than nine months. After almost four months, I was able to come home for three weeks. One of the happiest moments in my life was when Dylan was dropped off at my house, and he came running toward me with a huge smile on his face and his arms wide open. We held each other, neither of us wanting to let go. We had a bond that would withstand incredible challenges. We had a wonderful time together, but I could not help thinking, *How am I going to leave him again to finish my tour?*

Somehow I did it, with another tearful good-bye and wondering how many times a heart can break before it can't be healed. I just kept thinking, *Only one and a half months to go.* After I returned to the Middle East, time seemed to drag. I thought it would never end! But it did, thankfully, on June 23, 2004.

When I arrived home, I picked up Dylan at preschool. When he saw me, he had a look of relief on his face and literally fell into my arms. I vowed then and there that I would never leave him again.

I have since voluntarily released from the military to ensure Dylan and I will not be separated again. It was the best decision I've ever made. I have lost job security, but I have gained family security, which means so much more.

Sheryl McCormick

Framed

Two little pictures are on my fridge. Two girls, plastic framed and magnet backed, stare out at me from the mess of magnetic poetry and keepsake artwork. They look at me, and they always tell the same story.

I thought I would always be a stay-at-home mom; I had been for years, and I liked it that way. Then in the summer of 2005, I started working part-time for a literacy software company. I loved it. When they offered me a full-time position, I couldn't say no. We had just moved into a new—more expensive—town, and quite frankly, we needed the income.

So the fifth of September saw my little girls packed off to their new first and third grades, and me off to the office. The first few weeks were a painful adjustment—not to the work, but to the home life I was missing. Suddenly I left my girls at 8:30 AM and didn't see them till nearly 5:00 PM. My cell phone erupted in a volley of new-school bureaucracy: Health records! Vaccination records! Registration forms! Under which pile of must-dos had I buried today's requested forms?

I survived those weeks, somehow. And gradually life took shape, a life in which the evening hours were just as vital (and stressful) as the workday hours. The paperwork was filled out and handed in; the girls grew to love their after-school program and settled into their days well. And every day they returned home with a sheaf of notices, things for me to investigate and follow up on and do; and every day I scheduled my evening hours for this purpose (and the laundry, cooking, cleaning, and . . . but I digress).

One of those notices informed me about the school photo day. Without a doubt I picked up that notice, read it, and scribbled myself a must-do Post-it and tacked it in my planner. But as one day slid into the next and one emergency swallowed another, school photo day slipped from my mind. And disappeared altogether.

One day I had to leave early for work; as usual when that occurred, my mother-in-law readied the kids for school and dropped them off for me. It was somewhere around 11:00 AM when I spied a wrinkled Post-it sticking out of my planner, and a sickening wave of realization broke: it was school photo day, and I had sent my children to school completely and utterly unprepared. My world crumpled.

It wasn't just the photos. Obviously, a photo comes and goes. Never mind that this was their first year at a new school, that every other parent would take home a group picture of my unkempt daughters to place on their silver-trimmed mantels. But this was about more than that—this was about my working out of the house, about my not being there for them, about my having only so many brain cells, so much capacity for Post-it note retention, so much area over which to spread myself before the fabric started slowly, slowly to unravel.

And I unraveled. I pictured the outfits I'd wanted to send them wearing, color-coordinated and freshly pressed; the hairstyles that would highlight their features just right and the complementary accessories for their finishing touches. "I'm a bad mother," I wailed. "How could I forget something so huge?"

When I picked up the girls after school, I was not greatly reassured. Their hair was wild and windswept, not a hair-clip in sight. My youngest wore jeans and a white turtle-neck (with marker-enhanced sleeve cuffs). My eldest wore a flower-print shirt—nothing bad; nothing special. I shed more tears, mourned the prize photography that would not be.

And then I forgot about it, caught up in the next stack of notices, the next round of emergencies. Until one day the stack of notices contained two oversized envelopes: the photo verdict was in. But who could say what the sentence would be?

I tore open the envelopes—and the tears began again. But different this time. The photos were taken outside, and hair that could have looked unruly was sun streaked and windswept. Lowered arms hid offending sleeves; the jeans were well out of sight. An ordinary flower-print shirt turned the wearer into a garden fairy.

But more important than any of that was the joy I saw in the girls' faces. Those smiles filled the whole landscape from end to end. Those smiles said, "My life is pretty awesome, and I don't care who knows it!" So they weren't the sharpest, most stylish girls in the pack—but those smiles were enough for me.

And this is the story those pictures tell me every time I walk by the fridge. "You don't have to do everything, Mom," they say. "You don't have to be superwoman. In the end, you do the important things, and you do what really matters most—you care."

Joan Paquette

Mother: Guilty as Charged

From the time daughter Savannah was born, I had many decisions to make that would often leave me questioning if I had done the right thing. Whether it was a major decision—nurse or bottle-feed—or one as simple as the time limit I should allow Savannah to keep her sense of comfort—her beloved "pacey"—my mothering skills were under constant scrutiny.

One of my decisions, however, was never questioned: becoming a stay-at-home mother. Since the beginning of our marriage, my husband, Terry, and I agreed that if we were ever blessed with children, I would leave my elementary school teaching position for the career of "homebound" mom, especially during those early years.

Recently, another decision left me feeling much like a Benedict Arnold. After eighteen months of defending and praising my happiness as a stay-at-home mom, I rejoined the other side—the work force. Never mind that the job was only part time, my decision to accept a position at a local community college caused not only a controversy among various friends, but also within myself.

My stay-at-home mother friends asked me, "Aren't you happy being a stay-at-home mother?" My friends who worked outside the home gave me their support with smug smiles, as if to say, "We knew you would not stay content at home."

My once well-thought-out decision designed to allow me to enjoy the best of both worlds now made me feel guilty and confused. As I drove to my teaching assignment for the first time, I was still reevaluating my choice, all the while enjoying listening to the radio instead of Savannah's nursery rhyme tape.

Trying to convince myself that my main motive was to add to our family income, my mind also had other, more selfish reasons. Like many stay-at-home moms, I had missed conversation with adults. Lately, when I had the opportunity to talk with an adult, I found myself either refraining from using comments such as "That's okay, sweetie," or struggling for a topic of conversation (besides Savannah). Although I was still an avid reader, I didn't think my latest reading choices, *The Three Pigs* or *Goodnight Moon*, would be on anyone's book club list.

Slowly but surely, I was breaking a vow that I said I would never do to myself, my husband, or my child: Savannah was becoming my life.

Driving home after an enjoyable class, I reevaluated my statement to appease each set of friends, the stay-at-home mothers and those working outside the home. Then I began to feel that this silly battle of mothers could be summarized by the old statement, "The grass is always greener on the other side of the fence."

While a stay-at-home mother craves adult conversation, a working mother misses the babbling of her baby. While a stay-at-home mother feeds strained peas to an uncooperative infant and thoughts of a nice luncheon with other adults cross her mind, a working mother picks at her plate, worried that her finicky eater is not eating for the new caregiver. So instead of choosing sides, I thought that as members in one of the world's oldest occupations—motherhood—we should unite against a more important battle: the guilt of being a mother.

Friends warned that my life would never be the same once Savannah was born. I will agree that motherhood did change my life. Life has often become a struggle of my own personal needs against what is best for my child. More often than not, a mother's personal needs and desires are unselfishly placed a distant second. But as mothers, we should encourage each other to overcome the guilt of occasionally meeting some of our own personal needs.

After returning home from my class, I joined Savannah and my husband out in the yard. As Savannah clapped her hands and squealed in delight when we blew on dandelions, I was thankful for this moment together. Seconds later, she tried to eat the seeds instead of blowing them.

Whether it's blowing dandelions, deciding to stay at home, or working outside the home, motherhood is full of decisions. I often pray that I will choose what's right for Savannah; I also include a prayer to help ease my guilt as a mother—or maybe that's a bit too selfish?

Stephanie Ray Brown

2

"MOMMY" ON MY RESUME

To find joy in work is to discover the fountain of youth.

Pearl S. Buck

The Playground Lady

You think it can't happen to you. You are too suave. Too sophisticated. Too cool. But then it hits you like a well-aimed dodgeball, and before you know it, you've become your worst nightmare.

It always happens at fast food restaurant playgrounds. You are sitting there enjoying some random free time while your child scales the large plastic tubes that are remarkably similar to the hamster habitat you had as a kid. As you're imagining the addition of an exercise wheel, the first infraction takes place.

Someone is climbing *up* the slide.

You bite your lip. It's not your child. And didn't you climb up a few slides in your day? Sure did. At this point, you chuckle a little and decide just to lighten up.

Then the second infraction—blocking the ladder—begins to cause a domino effect of problems. Children can't get up the playscape. A cry goes up among the smaller children. Larger children prepare to take the ladder by force. You look around for the parent of the blockade leader, but everyone else is talking on his or her cell phone, pointedly looking away from the scene of the crime.

Then comes the final straw. A group of kids are climbing on the outside of the playground equipment in clear violation of posted rules! They are, as your mother always told you, about to break their necks!

Suddenly the Arnold Schwarzenegger of playground rule enforcement shows up, strides over, and peels children off the equipment. Then with horror you realize that it's you. You've become—the Playground Lady.

Of course, once it starts, there is no stopping it, no going back. Now you are deputized, immunized, and Mirandized. You are a woman on a mission. You stop the slide climbing. The blockade is removed, and normal flow returns to the bright red ladder. A rambunctious and persistent child begins to climb the equipment again and you toss that four-year-old a withering glance that sends him scrambling back into an orange tube tunnel.

You glance over at the tables, and everyone is still on their cell phones, oblivious to the fact that at least four broken necks have been narrowly averted.

Right about that point, you realize you have become the very authority figure you swore you'd never become. And it's a role you seem frighteningly good at.

So this is how it happens. This is how people go from being normal to crazed rule enforcers on the playground. Something deep inside snaps.

Maybe there's something in the french fries.

Finally your kid is worn out and you leave. By the time you hit the parking lot, you see a few kids climbing the slide again. Just as you are considering going back to lay down the law, you see a woman put down her cell phone and get up.

You smile as you put your car in gear. The torch has been passed.

Winter D. Prosapio

A Working Mom's Retirement Plan

Perhaps the greatest social service that can be rendered by anyone to this country and to mankind is to bring up a family.

George Bernard Shaw

"Mom" is a weighted word. Weighted with immeasurable love. "Working mom" is a title weighted with pure guilt. From the moment a baby is born, moms question their own decisions. Complete strangers feel they have the right to express opinions, and family members offer unsolicited advice.

In our society we refer to an employed dad as a mechanic, dentist, accountant, nurse, or banker, according to his occupation. Why is it then that we still refer to mothers who work outside the home as working moms?

When my children were small, I opted to work in a school so that I could be on the same schedule as my kids. I loved my job and still do, but truth be told, I aspired to be in the creative arts: journalism, photography, acting. A mom can dream, too. Often a working mom is so busy fulfilling her children's dreams she neglects her own.

Now that my children are adults, I realize I actually did achieve all of my aspirations. The pay scale was just different from what I anticipated. Although I never earned a journalism degree, I honed my writing skills each night. After I tucked my daughter and son into bed, I wrote page after page in the journals I kept for them—entries that made me laugh, cry, and wish they would never grow up. I completed not one, but two noteworthy "books," albeit handwritten and spiral-bound. I also wrote inspirational notes on bananas and tucked them into their lunch boxes. This tradition lasted until my son reached fourth grade. His teacher asked me to refrain when she discovered him passing my "love notes" to the girls. "Plagiarism!" I yelled at him.

Writers like feedback no matter what form the critique comes in. My critical acclaim came when I presented my children's books to them when they turned twenty-one. The reviews were laudatory and loud. If my "books" had made it to a publisher, I just know they would have been number one on the *New York Times* bestsellers list.

"Mom, I can't believe you wrote this. I did not do such a thing!"

"Mother! You have got to be kidding; I didn't know about that family secret."

My writing generated a lot of laughter, nostalgic tears, and accusations of embellishment. Every word was true, especially the closing comments: "As I look at you tonight, I want to hold you and keep you this age forever. I love you so much."

I didn't become a professional photographer, but I spent a fortune on film and equipment. Before digital cameras and video recorders, there were blinding flashcubes, popping flashbulbs, and canisters of film that had to be loaded into the camera and sent off to be developed. My interest in photography evolved into an obsession. I have large plastic tubs filled with loose photographs to prove it.

I gave up on categorizing and "album-izing" long ago. I have pictures of my children from the time they stretched my belly as big as an overinflated balloon to when they stretched their little arms wide as I asked, "How much does Mommy love you?"

I documented every milestone and achievement from the first official potty drop to the final handing off to their bride or groom. These days when I reach for my camera at family gatherings, my kids moan and reminisce.

"Remember the time we were on vacation driving through that desolate area in Arizona and Dad had to pull off the road so we could go to the bathroom?" my son asks.

"Yes, and Mom took a picture of us peeing!" my daughter shouts, so everyone a block away can hear.

"But it was only a rearview, distant shot; you couldn't see a thing." I defended my freelance photography. "You guys want a copy of that picture?"

I never had to dicker for publication rights or monetary compensation. I bought the film. I paid for the developing. I could send the candid shots to whomever could give me the highest exposure: their grandparents, girlfriends, and boyfriends. My photos would make Hollywood paparazzi green with envy.

Did I mention that I always wanted to be a performer? My dreams became reality the day my children were born. I cried on cue. When my daughter received her first immunization, I bawled right along with her. I sobbed all night with my little boy whenever he had an ear infection. I smiled like a drunken sailor when I dosed him with the pink liquid-magic that relieved his pain.

To get him to eat, I made up lullabies that I sang at lunch to the tune of *Mary Had a Little Lamb*: "Here's some yummy food to eat, food to eat, food to eat. Eat your yummy food today or you will have a long, long nap, long, long nap . . ." I could sing complete arias before they decided to chow down.

I deserved an Academy Award for my performances each Mother's Day when my children surprised me with runny eggs and burnt toast that even the dog refused. My acting ability improved through the years. I feigned happiness when my daughter's choices were way different from mine. I pretended it didn't hurt when my children turned into unrecognizable alien teens who freely expressed their opinions and tested me. I battled with wits, offered bits of wisdom, and I usually flunked the test of wills.

I never made it to Broadway or saw my name in lights, but I gave a stellar performance the year my daughter entered middle school. Her school bus driver was notoriously late in dropping off the children. When a student misbehaved, he would pull to the side of the road until order was restored. Consequently, the children were often late arriving home.

Some performances are best forgotten, but the day I acted out with the bus driver was so memorable my daughter's former classmates still mention it. When the traffic signal turned red and the bus halted, I bound from my car. As I stepped onto the bus, the driver radioed, "There's a crazy woman who has been behind my bus honking for half a mile, and she is coming on board."

"Release my daughter this minute! I've been worried sick about her safety. She is an hour late for her orthodontist appointment, and charges incur whether she shows up or not. What is the matter with you?"

I marched to the rear of the bus and escorted my embarrassed preteen down the aisle.

"Mom, what is the matter with *you!*"

"Take me, too," her friends shouted.

"Moms simply do whatever it takes for the sake of their children," I explained.

I've been a working mom for thirty years. I never found fame or fortune as a preschool teacher. I didn't become a professional photographer, and I didn't even grace the community theater stage. My pay has always been low, but my fringe benefits high. Arriving home at the same time of day as my children paid off in sticky hugs and sloppy kisses. I reaped dividends of unconditional love and shared quality time.

I don't have a personal retirement account, but I do have a future retirement plan. I plan to slow down. I plan to relax. I plan to sit with my grandchildren and share the wealth of memories, a pictorial account of my life as a working mom.

Linda O'Connell

"Even though I stay home now,
I still have a job . . . Career Mom!"

Learning to Smell the Roses

When I became pregnant with my first child, the question of whether or not I would stay home was an easy one. We were financially able, so I said my good-byes on my last day at work, fully confident that my coworkers' predictions of "You'll miss this" would not come to pass. I had a good job that I liked, but come on, who would miss the boring meetings, the unpredictable boss, the stress of deadlines? I had a vacation ahead of me with no end in sight. So long, suckers!

One afternoon during the first colicky month of my endless vacation, I was folding laundry and watching a talk show while my baby napped. "A stay-at-home mom works the equivalent of two full-time jobs," the guest psychologist said. I felt a surge of irritation and began folding the mountain of onesies faster. This guy had no idea what he was talking about.

At least when you worked outside the home you got lunch breaks. This life couldn't be compared with that of a mother working nine to five. There were no kudos, no raises, no goals to meet. There were no certificates handed out for "successfully completing ten diaper changes without getting peed on." There were no nights or weekends you could completely call your own. It never ended! Tears of self-pity stung my eyes. Why didn't all those parenting books I read ever say that *the work never ends*?

My poor husband became the victim of my postpartum resentment. Things only got worse when he accepted a job in New York City and we moved across the country.

"Guess where I had lunch today," he would say. (He seemed to say this every week after we first moved to the East Coast.) "The boss took us to one of the best restaurants in Manhattan!"

"That's nice," I would mumble. "I had the remains of a potpie Elizabeth left on her highchair tray. Ooh, and then I watched the same Barney video for the seventy-fifth time!"

At these moments I felt very ugly. I knew that I was being unfair. After all, the decision for me to stay home was mutual, and I was glad that we had made it. I knew that there were a lot of mothers out there dragging kids to day care at six in the morning and working at jobs they hated—mothers who would love to trade places with me. Then that self-defensive little devil on my shoulder would speak up. "Fair? Let's talk about fair. Is it fair that you went through nine months of discomfort, twenty hours of pain just to end up scarred for life from a C-section? Is it fair that he gets to socialize—*with adults*—at posh restaurants, sporting a stretch mark–free bod?" And so it went. I was in a cycle of resentment and guilt that was preventing me from enjoying life.

I remember the day that started to change. It was on a gloomy, housebound afternoon. All the blinds were open and snow was swirling outside, still a novelty to the "California Girl" in me. Elizabeth had just discovered that everything had a name. She was crawling around and pointing to things, asking, "That?"

"Remote," I would tell her. "Book. Baby monitor. Shoes."

I was only half-paying attention, my arms elbow deep in steaming water as I scrubbed bottles, my mind daydreaming. I was imagining the line of clothing I would design for new moms. No sizes allowed on the labels, and everything would be cream-colored to hide spit-up. Then I noticed that Elizabeth was quiet. I dried off my hands and walked into the other room, expecting to find her in a corner playing with the plunger. Instead, she was on her tippy-toes, craning her neck to see the center of the dining table. She had noticed a crystal vase of yellow roses, the only bright spot in the dim room. "That?" She asked, balancing herself while pointing at the vase.

"Flowers," I said. "Roses."

She continued to stare at the vase, a little Mona Lisa smile of wonder on her lips. I scooped her up and held her near the vase. "Want to smell them? See, smell." I put my nose to a bud and inhaled. "Mmm. Pretty." I held the rose to her nose, and she wrinkled it up, sniffing.

"Mmm!" she said, and grinned. This was followed by the other phrase in her vocabulary, "Oh, wow!"

For the rest of the day, Elizabeth went from object to object, trying out her new sniffing skill. She smelled perfumed pages in fashion magazines, wet wipes, pillows on the sofa, even a dirty diaper she grabbed when I wasn't fast enough. After each sniff she would say, "Mmm," and hold it out for me to smell. It occurred to me suddenly what a treasure I had in this moment. Throughout her life she would encounter scents, turning them into a collection of memories: the sawdust smell of the blocks in her kindergarten classroom, the tobacco-and-shaving-cream smell of her grandpa, the perfume she will wear on her wedding day. And someday the smell of her own baby's head nestled on her shoulder. But it all started here, on this day, when I taught her how to smell a rose.

When I put Elizabeth down for her afternoon nap—

"That?" "Blanket." "Mmm"—I noticed what wasn't there: The resentment was gone. The feeling of missing out on life was gone. A stay-at-home mom is a working mom, too. And the job is rewarding, even though you don't get that bonus every year or certificate of recognition, or even someone saying, "Thanks for ordering those bagels for the meeting. Good choice." I looked at my daughter's sleeping head on her blanket, her hair matted with bananas, just like mine. The surge of appreciation was like cold water on a burn. *But I get this*, I thought. I *get* this.

Tiffany O'Neill

A Mom First

As I was driving north on the 405 freeway toward Los Angeles on an overcast Monday morning, I suddenly had an overwhelming urge to turn around. *I'm on my way to work*, I told myself. *I have to go in today. I have a work deadline, and I can't just turn around and go home.* Besides that, I was nearly there. I could see the nine-story beige bank building I worked in just ahead. But the nagging whisper in my heart grew to a near audible inner shout, and I found myself turning around and driving south instead, toward the babysitter's house.

Home. I wanted to be home with Alicia, my ten-month-old daughter, more than anything. I longed to wrap my arms around her, read her a story, and tell her that life was something really special when there are people around who love you. I felt fresh tears burn my cheeks. What was *wrong* with me today?

I just needed to pick her up from the sitter and go home. All morning I hesitated taking my daughter to Pat's house. I was enjoying the morning with my daughter. We were having a great time during breakfast, laughing and playing. I hated having to end the moment and rush out the door to drop her off at Pat's. Thankfully, I had a great sitter. She was a wonderful neighbor lady who was a friend of my father and completely trustworthy.

When I'd dropped off my daughter that morning, Alicia had looked at me with an expression on her face that seemed to say, "You're abandoning me again?" With sadness in her shining blue eyes and a quivering bottom lip, she was a good girl and didn't cry as she waved bye-bye to Mommy. I was the one who ended up crying as I got behind the wheel and headed off to work.

Now, as I drove into the housing complex where the sitter lived, less than a half hour after I'd dropped off my daughter, I felt relief surge through me. I'd done the right thing. For today, anyway.

Over the next several days, the urge to be with my daughter grew stronger. I wanted to be there when she took her first steps, to remember the moment she said her first full sentence. I'd missed her first smile when she was three months old. The sitter had called me at work that morning to relay the news. I crumpled in my chair and broke into tears to the dismay of my concerned coworkers.

Over the next few weeks I got into my car and drove to work every day without turning back. I was in my early twenties and was proud that I was able to gather up my courage and go back to work after my daughter was born. I'd made a position for myself at my company. I was a hard worker who met my daily deadlines, then after the day was done, I picked up my daughter at the sitter's and spent the rest of the evening with her. I was a responsible homemaker, faithful wife, and loving mom. But nights and weekends with Alicia didn't seem like enough. My daughter was growing up fast and changing daily before my eyes. I felt I was seeing only half of all the beautiful changes she was going through and knew the most exciting experiences were yet to come.

Then the day arrived. The sitter called and told me the

"good news." Alicia was taking her first steps! "You should be here to see this, Kim," Pat said. After hearing all about it, I replied, "Yes, I should." I quietly hung up the phone and willed myself not to cry. That was the last time I would miss one of my daughter's milestones. I stood and gathered my things. I resigned that day.

And drove home.

The next several years were some of the happiest of my life. I spent all my time with my daughter. My husband completely understood. In fact, he relished coming home to his two girls every night, hearing of the latest news of Alicia's progress as she slowly grew from baby to toddler, then to a happy and well-adjusted young girl.

I'd done the right thing for me. Lots of moms can balance the work-mom situation without a hitch. I wasn't one of them. I took up baking, cooking, and sewing and loved staying home. When my son, Matthew, came along, my blessings doubled. I was thrilled to see my children grow, change, and learn. I was able to capture each and every special moment with them—moments that seemed to slip away all too fast.

When Alicia had a child of her own, I helped my daughter with her firstborn. I was able to experience my granddaughter Emi's first smile, first steps, and first laugh. But better yet was that I was able to experience all the special moments with Alicia, whose own special "first" moments I'd missed. And the best? Seeing Alicia's smiles and tears of joy at hearing Emi say for the first time, "I love you, Mama."

Kimberly Kimmel

"Your resume says you've got your Ph.D.,
your MBA and worked as a CFO and CEO
but your top listing is MOM?"

Happy Mother's Day

Mother's Day is traditionally accompanied by plaster handprints and bouquets of paper daffodils. If you're lucky, you may even be treated to a riveting breakfast in bed.

My plans to sleep in were interrupted by a chorus of clattering dishes from down the hall in my kitchen. Minutes later, a large plate, carried by a small child, appeared at my bedside. A pair of eyes peered over the edge. "Good morning, Mommy. I made you some breakfast."

I lifted the plate onto my lap and took note of the meal set before me. I had been presented with a slice of black toast, freckled banana, green-tinted boiled egg (leftover from Easter) and a cup of what appeared to be sawdust in water but smelled like herbal tea.

Putting on my best "mother of the year" face, I smiled and thanked my daughter. She stood and stared at me for a moment, then commanded, "Eat it." I stared back at her, hoping she didn't actually expect me to consume the early morning concoction. What I hoped was that she would leave the room so that I could hide the plate under the bed. Besides, I was saving room for brunch at the restaurant downtown.

A face complete with blinking lashes, a perfect grin, and rosy cheeks beamed up at me. I swallowed hard, trying to ignore her innocence. She handed me a paper napkin illustrated with two stick people, one tall and one small. Although they had no fingers, they appeared to be holding hands, and beneath their L-shaped feet were the words "Mommy and Me." That did it. A huge wave of guilt swept over me, and I prepared my taste buds for the inevitable.

When I bit into the toast, which had been slathered with butter-flavored vegetable shortening, it burst into a dozen pieces and landed around me on the bed. Loud crunches were emitted as I chewed, alerting the dog (aka garbage disposal in a fur coat) to rush to my bedside in hopes of retrieving a floor-bound treat. The boiled egg was equally crunchy—those bits of shell are hard to spot so early in the morning. And I hoped that Easter dye was to blame for the egg's suspicious green hue. I felt a bit of sympathy for the poor banana. It was impossible to peel, and its tropical brown flesh had to be squeezed directly from the organic wrapper into my mouth. It quivered at the back of my throat, daring me to swallow it. I then had no choice but to wash it all down with my cup of specially brewed tea. Bits of wayward chamomile, once constrained by a teabag, swam the perimeter of the cup. I lifted it to my lips, but did not drink. From the corner of my eye, I could see that I was still being watched. It was evident that my observer was enjoying the meal far more than I. I downed the tea in three quick gulps, which resulted in a full body shiver and goose bumps on my forearms.

"Was it good?" she asked. I opened my mouth to speak, but no words came out. So I simply nodded and faked a smile. The cup and plate were yanked from my hands, and as quickly as she had appeared, she was gone.

I leaned back into my pillows and sighed, trying hard to

retain the breakfast that could have easily been passed off as someone's poorly graded science experiment.

Seconds later, my budding chef returned. She climbed onto the bed next to me and held out a construction paper creation. "It's a book," she informed me. It was bound by bits of yellow yarn, strung through a series of punched holes, and the cover contained a lovely tissue paper flower.

I opened it and carefully admired all ten pages, each of which contained a drawing and captions, such as: "Thank you for making cookies on your day off." "You're the bestest mom ever." "I'm glad you take care of me." It became clear to me that someone in this house had actually been noticing all my hard work. Gee, I really was appreciated after all.

I thought back to previous Mother's Days and to all the presents that had been bestowed upon me, including rolls of Life Savers, bubble bath, bouquets of dandelions, half a bag of chocolate chips, an old hair ribbon, and a variety of homemade items. I was reminded that the sweetest and most precious gifts in a mother's life are not just those that are handed up to her by small hands, but those that are handed down to her from Heaven.

Ann Morrow

Weaving a Web of Wise Words at Work

I was very excited when I was hired as an advertising support clerk at the local newspaper two years after my son was born. I had enjoyed my tenure as a stay-at-home mom, but I was now ready for a change, ready to get back to work.

Not only was I thrilled to have my lifelong dream of working at a newspaper come true, but also I welcomed the challenge of learning new skills. These were both great incentives for going back to work, not to mention earning a paycheck again. But what I was most excited about was having a chance to engage in stimulating, informative, *grown-up* conversation.

For too long, my conversations had been decidedly one-sided and thoroughly nonintellectual. You just can't discuss the national news or theology or Shakespeare with a two-year-old child. My brain felt stymied by my drought. So, as I dressed for my first day on my new job, I was filled with anticipation. Surely the atmosphere at a newspaper was continually permeated with news. Surely opinions and orations, discussions and debates were standard fare, and I would have more than my share of intense, thought-provoking dialogues with my coworkers. I could hardly wait.

I sat at my computer, typing in real estate copy, but I had my ears pricked the whole time. All around me the phone reps discussed ads they had taken. I squirmed impatiently. When was the adult conversation going to start? I still felt shy, so I wasn't planning to put in my two cents right away; it would be fun to listen at first. Later I would dazzle my coworkers with my insightful observations.

It took a couple of days before it happened. One morning I came into the office and heard Carrie saying, "Of course, a lot depends on a person's upbringing, like where they were born, what part of the country, and so forth."

Debbie, resting her arms on the top of her cubicle, shook her head. "Yes, but some things are universal. Inherent."

"She's right," Jo put in. "Some things are just part of the human psyche."

I sat at my desk, listening happily. I had almost minored in philosophy at college. I remembered reading about the tabula rasa and a priori knowledge in my intro to philosophy class. And I'd also taken a cultural anthropology class. Finally! This was the kind of conversation I had looked forward to.

"People are taught in different ways around the world," Carrie argued. "Even here in the United States, there's a profound difference between how you're taught up North versus down South."

Chris chimed in. "Culture is a big part of it," she said. "Different cultures teach the same things in different ways. There's even differences between urban and suburban."

"You just know some things," Carrie said. "Like all children call their mothers 'Mama' or something equivalent to that."

"At first, sure. Then languages diversify," Chris said.

This was like being at an intellectual Wimbledon. I swiveled my head from one speaker to another, relishing the debate. My brain was kicking into gear, agreeing, disagreeing, disassembling, formulating arguments and rebuttals. I decided not to wait any longer. I got ready to jump into the exchange.

Then Carrie said, "But everybody knows the song is not 'The Eensy Weensy Spider.' It's 'The Itsy Bitsy Spider.'"

"Yeah, so tell your husband to get it right when he sings it to your little girl," Debbie said.

"He'll corrupt her," added Chris. "She'll go to kindergarten, and all the other kids will laugh at her because she sings the song wrong."

And we all began to sing 'The Itsy Bitsy Spider' with the hand motions, too, of course, as we'd done countless times with our children.

When we were finished, I turned back with a sigh to my computer. I knew for sure I was going to love working here.

Tanya Tyler

3

TAKING TIME
FOR ME

*In Genesis, it says that it is not good for a
man, to be alone; but sometimes it is a great
relief.*

John Barrymore

Authors' Note:

It's ironic—or more appropriately, prophetic—that this chapter, "Taking Time for Me," proved to be the most difficult to fill with stories. As any experienced mother knows and all new mothers quickly discover, days do not expand past twenty-four hours just because having an extra hour or two for oneself would be a good and healthy thing. Most mothers are quite happy to see many of their long days finally end before falling into bed, exhausted, yet fulfilled.

We imagine that finding the extra time to write a Chicken Soup story about the extra time mothers never seem to have for themselves was expecting a lot. We sincerely thank those of you who somehow managed to find that twenty-fifth hour in one of your hectic days so that you could share your stories with us.

Jumping In with Both Feet

Only do what your heart tells you.

Princess Diana

There is a time in life when one must look at the puddle being half full, not half empty.

My ten-year-old son, Shawn, is an optimistic kid. As soon as he turned nine, he told people he was "almost ten." When he has trouble mastering one of his pre-algebra problems (yes, pre-algebra is the new fourth grade math), he never gives up trying to figure it out. And he has his sights set on owning an exotic car someday, so he spends his free time learning as much as he can about these expensive cars, very much aware of the fact that the one he wants starts at a quarter of a million dollars. "No problem," he says.

One recent Saturday night when Shawn and I found ourselves walking across a nearly empty parking lot in the pouring rain, a huge smile appeared on his face. Wearing his good school shoes, he jumped into the middle of a very deep puddle and grinned at me, daring me to do the same.

The logical side of me was appalled that Shawn would

take a chance on getting in trouble by soaking his designer shoes right through to his socks. *Doesn't he appreciate that I work hard to make money to put those shoes on his feet, as well as a roof over his head and food in his belly?* my logical self questioned. Because I am a full-time author and writer, my husband and I budget years out at a time; since most of our income is based on book royalties, which are typically paid anywhere from a year to even three years after a manuscript is completed, we have to plan well and stick to that plan.

As I stood staring at my son in disbelief, I realized that his optimistic anticipation that I would jump into the puddle along with him was stronger than my pessimistic vision of the puddle ruining my good leather shoes and outfit. It was then that my life as a hardworking mom flooded into my reality. How many times had I begged off playing GameCube or building LEGOs with Shawn because of a manuscript deadline? How many times had I rushed him out of the car when dropping him at school to make it home in time for a conference call with a publisher? How many times had I said to him that we couldn't go to the movies because I had to edit a chapter for yet another book? It was then the most disconcerting question popped into my head: *Will the memories of my working hard to provide for Shawn and his older sister outweigh fond memories of acting silly and enjoying his childhood with him?*

Luckily it was raining hard, because if it wasn't, Shawn would have seen tears of gratitude for his lesson flowing down my cheeks. Without warning, I leaped into the puddle; delighted beyond belief, Shawn kicked water at me. I returned his water attack, and the two of us kicked and splashed and even pulled each other into deeper puddles, laughing until our sides hurt. Then hand in soaking hand, we skipped across the flooded parking lot to the ice cream store and treated our cold and shivering selves to double scoops of cookies-and-cream and mint-chocolate-chip ice cream.

So the next time you're with your kids and you come across a rain puddle, tempt yourself to look at it as not half empty, but overflowing with possibilities and fun. Then make a big, carefree splash. I guarantee you that they'll remember that moment for the rest of their lives, and so will you.

Dahlynn McKowen

Chat and Chew

"How was school today?"

"Fine."

"What did you do in class?"

"Nothing."

"Anything new?"

"No."

As any busy working mom will tell you, finding out what's going on at your child's school isn't always easy! So a group of us moms—bankers, doctors, lawyers, teachers, and nurses—formed a book club to get to know other moms in our community.

Once a month, over a relaxing glass of chardonnay and bites of crudités, we discussed the new principal, commiserated over the homework horror stories, and traded tips on how to complete that ridiculous science project that we, I mean, our children, had to complete by the next week. Sometimes we even discussed a book!

Of course, it wasn't long before the kids got curious about these book club meetings their moms wouldn't miss for anything. More than one asked, "Why can't we come?" Hmmmm.

Although all the moms relied on these meetings to socialize and share much-needed information with the other moms, everyone agreed it would be fun to set aside one meeting a year that the kids could attend. Because our children's ages ranged from toddlers to early teens, we wanted to pick a book that all ages—including ourselves—would enjoy. Though most of the children were old enough to read a book on their own, those who hadn't yet mastered their ABCs were thrilled to have their moms read to them. *Charlotte's Web* was a perfect choice.

The excitement on the night of the first parent/child book club meeting was palpable. Before discussing the book, the moms and children got to know one another better over a potluck dinner. It's amazing what the kids shared between mouthfuls of double cheese pizza. Listening carefully while nibbling on grilled chicken, the moms actually picked up enough clues to figure out the real answers to *How was school today? What are they doing in class? and What's new?*

Anxious to get to the main event, the kids cleaned their paper plates in record time and gathered in a circle. The moms were amazed at how responsible all the children were about reading the book (even more so than their parents!). One of the moms—a teacher, of course—got things going by asking a few open-ended questions about Charlotte and her famous web. From the youngest to the oldest, all the children participated and proudly gave an opinion. Some wished they could have a pig like Wilbur for a pet, and all unanimously agreed that their dinner had been much tastier than Charlotte's dinner of flies, bugs, and insects!

Still energized after a lively discussion about the themes of friendship, love, and caring, the older children continued their chatter about Charlotte, Fern, and Wilbur well into the make-your-own-sundae celebration. But as the youngest book club members started to yawn, the moms knew it was time for the evening to end.

Dinner and dessert might have been over, but every one of the busy moms left the meeting that night with quite a bit of food for thought.

Pamela Hackett Hobson

Making Memories

The best way to cheer yourself up is to try to cheer somebody else up.

Mark Twain

The leaves were at the peak of their color on an Indian summer day, and I was stuck working in my windowless cubicle and thinking about my sons. Have you ever thought about how easy it would be if we could drill a hole in their heads and stuff them with all the knowledge and wisdom we've learned? We all want to teach our children the joys and rewards of life and keep them from harm, but how do we do it? Every mother has days when she feels like her children's lives are slipping through her fingers, and today was one of those days for me.

Sure, I did all the normal things moms do: Cub Scouts, Boy Scouts, Pee Wee football, school plays, and so on, but I felt like I was missing something important. My oldest son was twelve and on the verge of that dreaded stage of adolescence. His hormones played havoc with his loving personality. He wanted to be an adult, but he still had the emotions and judgment of a child. It was hard to draw him out, and he didn't want to be hugged anymore. I felt him slipping away. My seven-year-old was full of the joy of being a child, but I was too busy working to see the world through his eyes. Before I could think about it or talk myself out of it, I asked my boss for a personal day without pay. Money was tight, and it would hurt our budget, but a day like this was a natural gift.

I didn't have any specific plan, but I knew I wanted to enjoy the day with my sons. I stopped in their principal's office and requested that they be released from school for the day.

When the boys came to the office, I winked and gently nudged them through the door. A huge grin spread across my face as they giggled and piled into the car. I remember feeling like I was shedding years and ready for fun.

As I pulled out of the parking lot, they asked me where we were going. I hadn't thought about it until then, but the inspiration came in a flash. "We're going to Starved Rock State Park to walk the woods and make a memory," I said. It was a place we had talked about, but never seemed to get the time to explore. My kids loved camping and anything to do with animals and nature. It was the perfect place to spend the fall day. The park ran along the LaSalle River in Illinois, and included miles of wooded nature trails and a famous rock. The leaves of the maple and ash were full of vibrant colors and just beginning to fall.

The kids chattered and asked questions the whole two hours it took to get there. They were excited about walking the trails and couldn't believe I was taking them on an adventure during a school day. I remember having a twinge of guilt about taking them out of school, but playing hooky together made it more fun and exciting for all of us. It was my way of telling them that our time together was more important than anything else.

As we walked through the woods, we talked about

everything that sprang into their minds. It was hard to keep up with the two of them as their thoughts jumped from one subject to another. I found out what interested them and what scared them in the dark. My oldest son even took the time to show his brother things he thought were important. We crouched over and studies some forest critters' tracks or droppings that he had found. They had a great time inventing stories about the woodland animals; watching them made me laugh and feel like crying at the same time. It was the first time in months that I had seen my oldest son so relaxed and happy.

Reading all the plaques along the trail, we learned about the native vegetation and the legends of the American Indian tribe that had lived along the river. We climbed the huge rock where the tribe, surrounded by their enemies, had either starved or leaped to their deaths rather than surrender. At the top I told them about the American Indian culture I had been fascinated with at their ages. We talked about places, people, customs, and religion as I shared other parts of my childhood.

The sight of the maples and ash trees in all their glory and the light reflecting off the river was gorgeous, but it was my children's laughter that put a lump in my throat. We sat on a rock, watching the boats on the river, when my seven-year-old looked up at me and asked, "What's making a memory?"

"It's doing something special that you'll remember all your life. We're making a happy memory." I put my arms around them and hugged them close. The oldest didn't pull away, and I felt like I'd broken through some adolescent barrier. That day I felt the closest to my children that I ever had.

The next evening I was doing the dishes and the boys were catching up on their homework when the phone rang. It was my youngest son's teacher. I felt like a child caught sneaking cookies. I was ready to apologize for taking him out of school, but she called to let me know that she thought spending time together was a wonderful idea. She told me how excited and proud my son was that his mom had taken him out of school just to be with him and his brother. She said he told the class about the American Indians, the woods, and all the animals that lived there. Instead of being upset because he'd missed a day, she said that he had probably learned more in that one day with me than he had in a week of school. She didn't want me to make a habit of it, but she said that more parents should take time to connect with their children. I told her I called it "making memories."

When I picked up my oldest son from Boy Scouts a few days later, several of his friends were waiting for me. They wanted to know if I had really taken him out of school just to be with him. I remember the grin on my son's face as he put his arm around me while I explained about making memories.

Don't get me wrong. I never made a habit of taking them out of school, because education rated highest on the list of things I wanted for my sons, but sometimes you have to seize the moment. Children grow so fast and time slips by before you know it's gone. You have to make an effort to listen to them and make special memories that show them how much you love them. They need to know that you cherish the time you spend with them. Sometimes that takes a conscious effort.

Although we all lose time in the busyness of life and working to provide for our children, sometimes we just have to say, "Wait a minute. Stop. I have to do this with my children." It can be as simple as taking time to make a batch of cookies. I found spending time with the children was a lot easier when they were little and I could hold them on my lap and give them a hug filled with love. It becomes harder as they grow older, so moms need to make special effort and be creative in finding special "memory makers."

Throughout the years, the boys and I made a lot of memories together. We had sleepovers, tree trimming parties, Halloween parties, campouts, and more, but their favorite memory is the day we spent at Starved Rock. My sons are adults now, and they never tire of telling this story at family gatherings. You don't need to spend money to make a memory; all you need is love and your imagination.

Jo Webnar

My Day Off

Thank goodness, today is Saturday, my day to rest, I thought as I snuggled under the blanket to enjoy the early morning silence. As a divorced mother of two girls, I looked forward to lazy Saturdays with nothing to do. Monday through Friday I had to be at work at 8:00 AM, and we were up early on Sundays for church. But Saturdays were *my* days—my days to sleep late.

Suddenly the silence was shattered by voices. "Wake up, Mommy, it's morning. Time to get up!" My daughters, Stephanie, age seven, and four-year-old Shelby, ran into the bedroom, jumped on the bed, and started pushing me up, laughing excitedly.

"Girls, this is Saturday." I complained. "I don't have to get up early."

"Yes, you do, Mommy," said Shelby. "You have to—" She stopped abruptly as her sister's hand clamped over her mouth.

"She means we're hungry, Mom. You have to fix our breakfast."

With a girl tugging at each hand, I allowed them to pull me out of bed. "Okay, do you want pancakes?" I said as I stumbled toward the kitchen.

"Yes, Mommy, pancakes," Shelby said. "I'm really hungry."

Throughout the morning, I noticed whispered conferences and giggling glances as the girls encouraged me to get dressed. They even offered to help me straighten up the house and do the breakfast dishes.

"What are you two up to?" I asked repeatedly.

"Nothing," they replied in unison, with eyes shining and mouths grinning from ear to ear.

Later that morning, the doorbell rang. Usually the girls raced toward the front door, but this time they hung back and waited for me. I pulled the handle and swung open the door.

"Surprise!" shouted the group of relatives congregated on the porch. My daughters jumped up and down, then began singing with the newcomers joining in: "Happy birthday to you, happy birthday to you. . . ."

"But my birthday is not until next week," I stuttered, "and I'm still in my pajamas."

"Well, let us in and get dressed," my sister said. "The ice cream is melting." We all laughed as they filed in.

"I'll just be a minute," I said as I retreated to my bedroom.

"Please, Mom, open your gifts first," exclaimed Stephanie. She danced around me with excitement.

"No, this is a party, and I want to look nice. Why don't you show Grandma where to put the cake, and I'll be right back."

When I returned to the living room, Shelby led me to the couch and placed a pile of presents in front of me.

"I'll help you open them," she said, tearing the paper from a small box. Between the two of us we opened the gifts, several of which had been purchased by their grandmother for the girls to give to me.

After the last one was opened, Stephanie announced, "Wait, we have one more for you, Mom."

Stephanie and Shelby disappeared into the bedroom

and came out carrying a grocery sack tied with a ribbon.

"This one is *really* from us," said Shelby. "We didn't have anyone help us with it."

I opened the sack. Inside was a dress that I hadn't worn in at least a year. As a matter of fact, the last time I'd seen it, it was in a stack of clothes destined for Goodwill.

"I guess you forgot about that dress," said Stephanie, "but we found it and knew you would be so happy to wear it again."

"Oh, I am," I said, hugging them close. "This is the best gift of all."

After we devoured the ice cream and cake, I told my mother that I was amazed that the girls had kept the party a secret.

"Not only did they keep it a secret," she replied smiling, "they planned the surprise party all by themselves. Stephanie called last week and gave us instructions on who to invite and what to bring. It was all their idea."

I shook my head in amazement as Mom continued.

"Stephanie and Shelby decided that you work too hard and you needed some fun in your life. What's more fun than a surprise birthday party?"

That night after I listened to prayers and tucked the girls into bed, Shelby asked, "Were you surprised, Mom?"

"Oh, yes," I replied. "I can't believe that you planned the party all by yourselves."

"Well," added Stephanie with a yawn, "it was hard, but it was worth it."

Yes, Lord, I thought as I looked at my daughters' sweet faces, *it's very hard, but it's worth it.*

Judy Spence

A Home of My Own

That's it! I am done, finished, kaput. It is over. I have put up with it for years and years and years, and I am not going to put up with it anymore. I am getting my own apartment. My very own apartment. There will be one key. My key. There will be absolutely nothing crusty or unidentifiable on any of the furniture in my apartment. The dark wood will gleam richly. Delicate, precious objets d'art will be placed tastefully and to their best advantage here and there with no fear that they will meet violently with an unexpected flying object of any kind—not a football, not a shoe, not a cat. Nothing will fly in my apartment but my hopes and dreams.

All my dishes will match, and none of them will be from Taco Bell. They will be lovely, delicate bone china. Hand painted. Antique. I will never find them in the backyard. I won't have a backyard, but if I did have one, I would never find my dishes there being used as a pill bug nursery.

I will have a brand-new toothbrush that I will know with absolute certainty has never been used for anything but my own teeth. Because sometimes I am not so sure about my current toothbrush. With wide-eyed innocence everybody always denies using it, and then just when I start to believe them and relax a little, somebody will pipe up with, "Wait a minute! I thought I was green! I was green last time! Then who has the purple one?" I hate that conversation.

After I get my apartment I will go shopping. I will buy a pair of nail clippers, tweezers, Scotch tape, pens. No! One really good pen. Some eye shadow that will never, ever, ever be used as camouflage paint, *no matter what*! I will buy special apartment clothes. They will never be worn by anybody else. These apartment clothes will be mine, and they will be laundered appropriately.

The clothes I have now? Well, just let me try to buy something nice. The minute my back is turned, someone in this house will root it out—ignoring the huge pile of dirty laundry that is a permanent fixture on the floor in front of our washer—root it out, I tell you, and throw it into the washer with a load of dishtowels and a quart of bleach and then into the dryer set on "nuclear holocaust" for *four hours*. And then whoever has done all this most recently will get their feelings hurt if I complain. "I was just trying to help!" No, you wretched torturer of fine fabrics, you were trying to ensure being grounded from using the washing machine. What a twisted joke! You know you have sunk to the very depths, the slimy, lightless chasm of motherhood, when you hear yourself saying, "That's it, young lady! No more laundry for you! Don't even think of it!" Oh, they're wily, they are!

I will glide through my apartment admiring it. Barefoot. Because there will never have been a LEGO in that apartment, ever.

Then I will take a very long hot bath. It will be long because nobody will be there to bang on the door and yell, "What are you doing in there?" "Do you know where my other G.I. Joe sock is?" "How come they say it's hot enough to fry eggs on the sidewalk, because I tried it *twelve times* and nothing fried?" "Can Johnny come in and see your appendix scar?" "Do we have anything good to eat?" It will be hot because I will be the first, last, and only person to use the hot water. When I am finished, who knows? The sky is the limit! I will tweeze if I want to tweeze because my tweezers will be where I put them, where they belong. And they will catch and pluck each tiny hair, no matter how wispy and fine, with exquisite precision because they will never have been used as a screwdriver or a bug immobilizer or a brother pincher. They will be only what they were meant to be. And they will be mine! And my tweezers and I will live the whole of our secret lives together happily ever after.

Huh? Nothing, honey, just dozing. The tweezers? I don't know. Did you look in your tackle box?

Elizabeth Bussey Sowdal

Earning the Privilege of Being Sick

I make my way into the kitchen with the unsteady gait of someone who has spent the last day and a half in a haze of sickness, drifting in and out of sleep. I wobble into the empty kitchen. My husband is at work, the kids at school, and I have called in sick for another day. This is the first I have ventured out of bed.

An empty fast-food bag is on the counter. I guess they had Wendy's for dinner last night. If I had the energy or inclination, I could probably study the wide assortment of crumbs and drips that line the counters to recreate every snack and beverage consumed by the rest of the family while I was flat on my back. But I don't.

I open a cabinet and give some thought to trying instant oatmeal. My queasy stomach tells me no, but not before I notice a shelf full of Hostess treats. My husband must have made a trip to the grocery store. At least I know no one is starving.

Wait! My eyes dart to the fishbowl, where Jeffrey II (at six and one-half years of age, now a few months older than his namesake, Jeffrey) is swimming in desperate circles. Someone is hungry. It's been a long time since anyone other than me has thought to feed the fish. Apparently, no one thought this time either. I give him an extra shake of flakes.

I can tell the dog was not forgotten. I know because her bowl is overflowing with food, some of which has escaped to the floor, scattered around the bowl in an interesting landscape of peaks and valleys.

I stagger into the dining room, where I see four of my daughter's sweatshirts in an appealing array on the table and chairs. Katy, age twelve, wears a sweatshirt to school just about every day. I can't decide whether the pile includes shirts she has worn or shirts she decided against wearing. Probably both.

I notice my son's winter jacked slumped over a chair. I know the temperature outside is hovering around twenty degrees. I wonder what Mikey, age fifteen, is wearing.

I head into the living room, my sights set on the sofa, where I aim to spend the day in repose. I note two days of newspapers piled unceremoniously on the floor. Quilts and pillows are here and about, testimony to a cozy evening spent watching television and reading. I stumble into the sofa, tripping over my husband's shoes on the floor next to it.

The phone rings. I answer the portable, which I have wisely transported along with me into the living room.

It is Grandma. Her son (my husband) has called her from work asking for her breaded chicken recipe, which he plans to make for dinner.

"I forgot to tell him to season the chicken first," she tells me.

I assure her I will pass along the message.

The call reminds me that my son Matt, eighteen, had telephoned me from college the previous day. Alerted online by his dad that I wasn't feeling well, he called to see how I was doing. It was nice to hear his voice sounding so solicitous.

In fact, the rest of the crew has been pretty solicitous, too. Bringing juice and tissues, popping heads into the sick room to inquire if I needed anything.

It occurs to me that I have passed some important milestone of motherhood. After all, it wasn't that long ago that I was not allowed to be sick. The complications, extra arrangements, and added concerns always convinced me that it was just easier to keep going, no matter what.

But I can see from the artifacts scattered around my empty house that my family has handled things just fine without me. Maybe not exactly the way I would have, but fine nonetheless. I grab the remote control and settle in on the couch.

After years of service, I've earned my sick leave.

Mary Vallo

"Gee, Mom, I'm sorry you're sick.
But can't we hire a sub?"

The Contract

I had always heard there was nothing better than being your own boss. After working in the media for eighteen years, I decided to go it alone as a radio talk-show host and freelance writer. But having a home-based business was more difficult than I imagined. Especially because my daughter stayed home with me all day.

"Mommy!" cried three-year-old Micah from the kitchen.

The click of my heels on the tile echoed down the hall. My mother would be here any minute to watch Micah while I attended a morning meeting. Thank goodness for Mom. Now retired, she usually could babysit with a little notice. She even kept Micah overnight on Fridays while my husband, Michael, and I enjoyed some time as a couple.

Micah sat at the kitchen table. Strawberry milk mixed with globs of oatmeal surrounded her. "I made a little mess," she admitted as she scrunched up her nose. "Sorry."

I grabbed a dishcloth and stifled a sigh. "It's okay, sweetie. Let Mommy help."

As I bent over to clean the goop off the floor, Micah leaped from her chair onto my back. "Giddy up, horsie!"

"Not now, Micah." I tried not to sound annoyed. As she

slid down, she gave me a big hug around the neck and a kiss on the cheek.

Ding-dong.

"Grammy, Grammy, Grammy." Micah darted for the front door.

"Good morning," chirped Mom.

I threw the dishcloth in the sink, grabbed my briefcase, and headed toward the door. "Thanks for coming. The kitchen floor is slick, beware," I announced as I hugged Mom.

"Might want to change your jacket," Mom said, pointing to clumps of oatmeal on my shoulder.

I sprinted to my bedroom. Nothing new for me; I was always running, literally and figuratively. Interviewing guests, meeting with advertising clients, stopping by the store for more groceries, cooking meals, and taking care of the house, Michael, and Micah left little time for anything else—or anybody else. Including me.

We had photographs, so I knew I must have had a life before I started my own business and became a mother, but I could barely remember what it was like to sleep in on the weekends, linger over lunch with a friend, or lose myself in a good book.

Because I mainly worked at home and Michael's business had flexible hours, I figured caring for Micah all day wouldn't be that hard. And it wasn't, unless I wanted to do something else. Trying to squeeze in work when she slept or when I could coordinate with Mom or Michael to watch her was hectic. There was definitely no downtime for me.

Now with a jacket sans breakfast stains from a three-year-old, I kissed Micah and hugged Mom good-bye. "Hey, your birthday is this month." I suddenly remembered. "Think about what you want."

"I already have an idea, but it's a little out of the ordinary," Mom answered with a smile. "Julie Andrews is coming to town. Think we could get tickets?"

"That sounds easy enough," I replied, shutting the door. After all, I worked in the media. Event tickets were my specialty.

A couple of Saturday evenings later, Daddy and Micah had a date while Mom and I went downtown to the Civic Center. On the drive into the city, we chatted like school-girls. Before Micah was born, we often did things together, but now our attention centered on Micah. I'd forgotten how much I missed having my mother all to myself, and planned to enjoy it, even if it was for only a few hours.

As I sat in the darkened theater, I breathed deeply. So this is what it feels like to be relaxed. My responsibilities at work and home floated out of my mind. I got a faint glimmer of who I used to be—before my business, hus-band, home, and daughter consumed my time.

Sure, my life was everything I'd hoped for. But I craved some "me" time. Until now, I was unaware that I desper-ately needed a night off. I enjoyed myself so much that it almost felt like my birthday instead of Mom's.

"That was so much fun," said Mom as we walked to the car. "Let's do something like this again."

The next week, while on the phone with a client, he negotiated: "I want to buy the radio spots, but I want them for a different rate."

Eager to make a deal, I agreed. "Okay, write in the price you suggested, fax the contract back to me, and I'll take a look at it."

Wish I could strike a bargain like that! I thought, hanging up the phone. I leaned back in my desk chair. *Just what would I negotiate if I had a contract?*

That evening I cooked all of Michael's favorites: meat loaf, corn, mashed potatoes, rolls. I even got a cake from the in-store bakery.

"What's the occasion?" he asked, suspicious.

I smiled sweetly. "I decided that I want to start cooking more often."

After I put Micah to bed, I found Michael in front of the television. "Honey, I want to be a better wife and mother, so I came up with this." I handed him a sheet of paper—a contract that outlined all the things I was already doing: working, cooking, housework, shopping, errands, caring for Micah. At the bottom I had only one request: Saturday night off.

"It's a small concession, don't you think?" I asked.

Michael nodded. How could he refuse when everything I did was listed right there in black and white?

I now sometimes spend Saturday evenings at dinner with Mom or friends, but mainly, I just hang out in the bedroom and read. Michael makes sure Micah eats dinner, takes a bath, and gets to bed. And I have the night off to do whatever I please.

Every mother needs to negotiate a little time off. When my contract comes up for renewal, I plan to ask for Tuesday afternoons off, too!

Stephanie Welcher Thompson

4

ENLISTING EXTRA HELP!
Day Care, Housekeepers, Husbands, Grandparents, Kids, and More

There is . . . nothing to suggest that mothering cannot be shared by several people.

H. R. Schaffer

The Choice

It was exactly like everyone said it would be. The birth of my son, Benjamin, was the most exhilarating, wonderful joy I have ever experienced. I wouldn't even let him spend a night in the hospital nursery; I couldn't bear for us to be apart.

Faced with the typical new-mom challenges of sleepless nights, endless laundry, the slow deflating of my body (it was as if someone had pumped me full of air—I had been a huge, pregnant woman), I was tired and cranky during those first few months. And though most days I looked like I had walked through a wind tunnel and emerged with spit-up on my tattered T-shirt, I was in awe over the immense love I felt for my son.

Amid the insanity of learning to care for an infant, I was also trying to stay on top of my two businesses. Business owners don't get maternity leave, but I knew that when I made the decision to say good-bye to corporate America and follow my dreams.

My first business was a bookstore I opened in Sacramento, California. Once that was running smoothly with a staff to handle daily operations, I launched BusinessInfo Guide.com, a directory of resources for entrepreneurs. I also published two books and wrote dozens of articles for magazines—all in a span of three years. I was working twelve-hour days and loving every minute of it.

Then we decided to have a baby. When friends warned that having a baby changes everything, I replied smugly, "It doesn't have to if I don't let it." I assumed that I could just prop Ben up on my desk and keep working. He would be my sidekick, making my workday even more enjoyable. Today I can only laugh at my naïveté.

It took awhile to realize my dilemma. Like all infants, Ben slept for the majority of the first couple of months. I thought I had the perfect plan and gave thanks to my decision to work for myself. I certainly couldn't prop him up on my desk in a cubicle in corporate America.

I was able to get some work done during the day and planned to stay up late to catch up on the rest. But there was a glitch in my plan—by the end of the day I was a zombie. With an average of four hours of sleep per night—and we're not talking about consecutive hours—I could barely spell my name by 6:00 PM.

Soon, the time between Ben's naps began to extend. I felt torn between wanting to spend quality time with my son and finding time to tackle the mounting stack of work awaiting me in my home office.

That's when I realized I had to make a choice.

As much as I hated to admit it, I was not superwoman. I had to either give up my businesses or get some child care.

In the midst of the decision-making process, I joined a mom's group and noticed that many of the women had screen names like "Madison's Mommy" and "Mom-to-Maya." I was proud to be Ben's mommy, but I was also Stephanie, a wife, a writer, and a businesswoman. The fact that I didn't want to be exclusively identified as "Ben's Mommy" left me wondering if I was missing some sort of mommy gene. To make matters worse, many of the moms who didn't work left me feeling guilty about the fact that I still did.

I loved my son more than anything on this earth, but I also derived a lot of satisfaction from working. Sure, as a mom I worked hard, harder than I had ever worked before, but the days were bleeding into one another, and I was losing my sense of self.

The guilt was overwhelming. What kind of mother doesn't want to spend every waking moment with her child? Was I a horrible person? Did I even deserve to have this gift in my life? I had several working mom friends who would give their right arms to stay home with their children. But I wanted to have my cake and eat it, too. I wanted to spend time with my son and also have adult conversations.

At the same time, I was wrestling with another dilemma. "I can't stand the thought of leaving him with a stranger," I confessed to my husband through loud sobs. "I had no idea I would feel this way."

"You need to make a choice," he told me. "I will support whatever you decide to do, but it's up to you."

With trepidation, I began interviewing day-care providers, but nobody seemed right. I wondered if I was somehow sabotaging myself and if anyone would ever be good enough to care for Ben.

Finally, my husband had had enough. Ben was almost five months old, and I could barely keep it together. The mounting pressure of neglected work on top of the demands of daily life was turning me into a raving maniac, and it was my husband who suffered my wrath. I had incredible patience all day with my fussy baby, but I bottled up the frustration and smacked my husband with it the minute he returned home from work. I also realized that I was subconsciously blaming him because I wanted him to fix it for me.

Then one day I interviewed yet another day-care

provider, and to my surprise, I actually liked her. She interacted so well with the children that I wanted to take notes—I could learn from her! I called the licensing department and checked her references; twelve years in business and nothing but good news.

"I want to keep working," I finally told my husband. "I don't think I'm cut out to be a stay-at-home mom." The words hung in the air like toxic smoke.

"I never thought you were," he replied.

"What does that mean?" My guilt turned to anger.

"You love working; you have since the day I met you. I know you love Ben, but you deserve to have both if that's what makes you happy." I knew he would find a way to fix it. That was exactly what I needed to hear.

In the end, I decided to put Ben in part-time day care, about thirty hours per week. It was a good compromise, allowing me the satisfaction of a productive workday, while still providing us plenty of time together.

Of course, the first day I dropped Ben off at day care was traumatic. The two- and three-year-olds gathered around us gleefully and chanted, "Ben's here. Ben's here!" Ben's face lit up; he loved looking at all those little people. He barely noticed when I began to make my way toward the door. I told myself it was good for him, too. He would enjoy the stimulation. It was for just a few hours.

As I reached for the door, the day-care provider called out, "Don't worry, he'll be just fine." Tears erupted from a place deep inside of me, and I looked up at her slowly, embarrassed by my lack of control. In that moment I realized that it wasn't lack of control that brought me to tears, it was the love of a mother. Ben's mommy.

"I know," I said. "And I will be fine, too."

Stephanie Chandler

Another Calling

Obstacles are those frightful things you see when you take your eyes off your goal.

Henry Ford

Leaving the work force to stay home with my kids for a while held unexpected benefits. One was a complete reevaluation of my career choice. Before our first child was born, my husband and I had it all figured out. We knew we wanted three kids. We'd have them close together, then when the youngest started school, I'd jump right back into my advertising career. The day I packed up my desk, that's how I left it with my coworkers. "Ya'll hold down the fort. I'll be back in a few years." But after fifteen years at home, I hope they've stopped waiting.

Advertising had been a perfect fit for me. Then a funny thing happened. A nurse I'd never seen before placed an eight-pound baby girl in my arms and, at that moment, I reevaluated everything. Before then I'd known exactly what mattered in life—making money and having fun. But as I lay in that hospital bed and looked into Haley's eyes for the first time, I was surprised to realize that global warming and the arms race were now my problem. In that same instant, I realized I didn't give a hoot how best to extol the attributes of the new Toyota Sienna. In the grand scheme of things, it just didn't matter.

Fast forward seven years and two more babies. Advertising is the farthest thing from my mind as I spend my days with Big Bird and *The Runaway Bunny*. Now, mamas have to be careful what they say. There's always an audience, one who takes things quite literally. And one day when I mused something like, "I always wanted to be a writer," I suddenly found three pairs of eyes looking up at me as if to say, "But, Mama, you always tell us we can do anything we set our minds to." It was one of those life-changing moments. I knew I either had to put my money where my mouth was or watch my children grow up and settle for less than what they really wanted.

Did I want to be a writer? I wasn't sure. But looking into those eyes, I knew I was about to give it my best shot. I sat my girls down, seven-year-old Haley and five-year-old Molly, while two-year-old Hewson squirmed on my knee. I explained to them as best I could that Mama wanted to be a writer. I asked if they wanted to help me. They did. I told them it wouldn't be easy. We'd probably work a long time before we ever saw anything I wrote published in a magazine or newspaper.

We made a list of the things we'd need to get started. Within a week I had a makeshift office set up in the laundry room, letterhead, office supplies, and a book to walk me through the beginning process. Even if I never saw my name on a byline, I figured this was a golden opportunity to teach my kids a lesson in determination and goal setting. We decided that because we knew we'd receive many rejection letters before anything was accepted and published, we'd welcome each one as a step closer to our goal.

I made sure they saw every essay and query for an

article I sent out. Molly liked to hold the big yellow envelopes in her hands and say a prayer over them before she put them in the mailbox. We didn't have to wait long before the rejections started rolling in. Sometimes several a day. We taped each one to the laundry room wall. Haley read them out loud to her brother and sister: "Does not meet our editorial needs at this time. Hope you have luck placing it elsewhere." They took turns taping the letters on the wall. Months went by. We filled one wall, another, and started on the third. *What a visual for my kids,* I thought. Twenty, thirty years from now, when they're faced with a challenge, a goal, an obstacle, they'll close their eyes and picture that room, ceiling to floor with rejection letters, and their mom bent over the computer plugging away.

I have to admit there were days when sentences like "We appreciate you thinking of us but unfortunately . . ." and "We realize the time and effort you put into your submission. However . . . ." cut me to the quick. No matter how eloquently a rejection is worded, it's still rejection, and some days it's harder to take than others.

But the girls celebrated each one. "One step closer, right, Mama?" "Wow, we're filling up another wall. Won't be long now!"

One day a friend showed up with a large cork board. She nailed it on the remaining wall. In the middle she pinned a letter she'd written telling me what a terrific writer, mother, friend, and Christian she thought I was. I couldn't have needed it more. After that I took other encouraging letters I received and pinned them on the board. The kids drew pictures of me at the computer and wrote encouraging messages: "Mom is a grat ritr!" and "We ar goin to sel a store soon!" When the rejection letters started to get to me, I'd turn my chair toward the board and drink in all that encouragement until I had the energy to get back to work.

Eight months into the process the phone rang. It was a sale! A month later another! Two months later another! We had a party and ceremoniously pulled all the rejection letters off the walls. They'd served their purpose. It's been eight years now, and there are still lean months. But I'm happy to report that the world of advertising will have to keep going without me. Haley, Molly, and Hewson's mommy is a writer now.

I was thinking the other day that I might like to take the next step and write a book. But something tells me I'd better keep that idea to myself—for a while anyway.

Mimi Greenwood Knight

The Button

If either of my sons has the ambition or calling to become president of the United States, the American people can rest assured that they will not have to worry about him pushing the "button." In fact, I fear that my sons' future wives will be in for a hard time getting them to push any button, unless, of course, it is located on a television remote or a video game controller.

The other day, my husband, Larry, looked at me rather strangely when I asked the boys to check the wash and became rather specific in my instructions.

"Brent, did you start the laundry?"

"Yes, ma'am. The whites are done."

"Good. Have you switched the loads?"

He nodded.

"Did you tell your brother to push the button?"

That is when I noticed Larry raise his eyebrow.

Brent disappeared with the wonderful chore of telling his younger brother what to do, and the extreme pleasure of being able to add, "Do it *now!* Mom said."

A few months ago, whenever the boys cleaned their rooms, I found four loads of laundry and "dirty clothes" that were still attached to hangers deposited on the bathroom floor. Larry and I decided that the kids would be in charge of the laundry. Brent would be in charge of sorting and washing. Brad would dry and fold.

I had a brief moment when the clouds actually parted and a sparkling beam of heavenly light and angelic voices surrounded me. I thought in anticipation about coming home to the hum of the washer and dryer, clean clothes, towels, and blankets folded neatly and waiting to be used. *Ahhhh, heaven.* Every mother knows that laundry never stops, and the thought of not having to think about that particular chore was a wonderful fantasy.

Fantasy. That was the right word. I should have remembered that just because we had put the children in charge of something doesn't necessarily mean we can forget about it.

I smiled at my husband even as we heard Brad's voice rise in the hallway. "Okay, Brent, I'm doing it! Quit telling me to push the button. I'm pushing it!"

Larry's raised eyebrow invited an explanation.

"Apparently," I began, still smiling, "it is Brent's job to transfer the wet clothes from the washer to the dryer, but not to push the button. Brad is supposed to push the button and then set the timer. If Brent forgets to tell Brad he has switched out the loads, or if Brad decides he'll push the button "in a minute," I come home from work to wet clothes in both the washer and dryer and no dry towels for morning."

I sighed. "I am the coordinator. Apparently, it is my job to make sure they communicate and that the button gets pushed."

Larry smiled at me and called the boys into the room.

"Brent, from now on, you are in charge of all the laundry. Brad, your job is now the dishes."

Brad's eyes became as big as the plates he was now in charge of washing. (Did I mention that we don't have a dishwasher?)

"If you can't work together, you'll work alone and do more work."

That sounded great to me. (I love my husband.) It was a victory for Mom and Dad—teaching our young men the responsibility of taking care of a home, while giving Mom a break from the two chores that never seem to be completed.

Now I can fantasize about coming home to a clean kitchen and fresh laundry. I am picturing my dishes stacked neatly in place in my cabinets, the laundry done and put away. No buttons, no arguing, no problems. Can't you just hear those angels singing? No, don't spoil it, I'm still dreaming.

I'll find out soon enough what buttons I'll have to push to keep those chores completed.

Vanessa Ann Cain

That Ugly Thing

Work situations might call for computers, but I could not think of a single reason to have one at home. After using it all day at work, why would I want one of those drab, unappealing, electronic boxes and accompanying paraphernalia in my home, my nurturing oasis?

But when we ended up with one, what choice did I have? I succumbed.

The computer sat on a corner-tucked table, the printer hooked up neatly on a shelf below. I shopped dutifully for the best prices on printer cartridges and paper, and set about making use of the ugly thing. What in the world would I do with a computer? It was all I could do to juggle school and work schedules, grocery shopping, and laundry.

My son took the lead, making it quickly evident that even two-fingered keyboarding produced nicely finished reports and legible homework. We laughed as we input our Christmas card list in the middle of summer, but surely found it handy to take printed labels on vacation, which made sending postcards a snap. I began writing long letters to distant family members, making detailed to-do lists, and digitizing telephone trees for various organizations. My fingers were burning up the keys, but I still regarded that PC as an amusement rather than a useful tool.

As utilities, gasoline, and grocery costs climbed, I looked for economical shortcuts. When I cut back expenses, groceries were my first target. Two competing chains in our area were running games that promised great rewards, but I saw them cover with escalating prices.

I waited until early on a Saturday morning after a busy workweek. Clipboard in hand, I visited both food stores and the buying club. Aisle by aisle I went, noting item number, package size, and price. Up one shelved row and down the next I scribbled on my notepad as I walked. I must have appeared to be an employee making an order or taking inventory. Ha!

Back home I rushed to the keyboard. Quickly I sorted the items into most frequently purchased and which store offered the best price. Prioritization came next, with the most nutritious first, followed by treats, with once-in-a-while splurges bringing up the rear.

While I was at it, I devised a menu plan that utilized leftovers and listed items that dovetailed with the growing shopping list. The completed document hung on the refrigerator, a fairly compact list with blank check boxes. All a family member had to do was make a check mark on the list upon finishing the last of any pantry or refrigerated item. No more discoveries of empty spaces in the cupboard *after* I'd finished buying groceries.

Shifting shopping responsibilities gave this working mom a break. When it came time to shop, anyone could do the stocking up and stay within the budget. Family cooperation rose to an all-time high, and that ugly computer earned a place in my home life.

Maryjo Faith Morgan

Dear Working Mom

From what we get, we can make a living; from what we give, however, we can make a life.

Arthur Ashe

You just left your child with me. As I opened the door for you and your son, I saw your forehead scrunched up in worry even as your lips tried to smile. In your eyes I saw the pleading, *make this easy for me.* I couldn't tell if you were sending the thought to your boy, so that maybe he wouldn't sob as soon as he saw me this time. Or maybe you were silently asking me to work some day-care magic and make him content to be here without you. Or maybe it was the end of a prayer you had been praying since you went to bed last night.

I have a special perspective working as a day-care provider. I have left my children with others and others have left their children with me. I have shut the door on my son's wails and then cried all the way to work, and I have sat and rocked a child who just heard mommy shut the door.

I understand. I am here with your son. I can help the sadness I see on his face, but I want to ease your sadness, too.

Leaving your child with me does not make you a bad mother. His crying when you bring him does not mean you are a bad mother. Your son cries when you bring him to my house because he wants to be with you as much as you want to be with him, and he doesn't have the words to tell you. He makes it hard on you because he loves you best. You are his world.

I will never be as good as you are at kissing away the boo-boos, and when he snuggles in for a story, my lap will never be as comfy as yours, but he does have fun at my house. And what's more, he is learning how to make friends and many socialization skills. He is learning independence at my house.

So go ahead and call me when you get to work—you'll hear no crying in the background. Because the crying stops before your car leaves my driveway. He starts playing with his friends by the time your car turns off my road. Before you eat your lunch we've been singing and laughing.

I'm sorry today was not easy on you—again—but I promise that it will get better. One day he will smile and wave as you leave. One day he will walk through my door on his own with a big smile, and you will have to call him back saying, "Don't I even get a kiss good-bye?" And then he'll walk back to you with big heavy steps, his head tipped to the side, and he'll sprint away as soon as your lips touch his cheek. One day he will cry when you arrive to pick him up because he just started playing with his "bestest" friend in the whole wide world. One day . . .

I wish I had day-care magic to make "one day" come sooner. Until then, please remember that you are doing something wonderful by going to work—for you and for him—and it will get better. For now, just think of his cries as his saying, "I love you, Mommy!"

Love, Your Day-Care Provider

Mindy Potts

You Are So Special to Me

You have loved me since you met me
I was only five weeks old

When mommy went to work
You were there for me to hold

I thank you for your loving arms
That keep me safe all day

For taking care of me so well
In your special loving way

I know you're not my mommy
Though you treat me as your own

I am so blessed to have you
And will love you till I'm grown

I know I'm just a baby
And I need you by my side

To teach me how to do things
And which rules I must abide

I think you are my special angel
Your wings I cannot see

For all these things and more you do
You are so special to me

Christina Guzman

POSTSCRIPT: *Being a working mom it is such a blessing when you find someone who cares for and loves your child as much as you do. I dedicate this poem to all the day-care providers who give so much of themselves to the children they care for. Every day I thank God for blessing me and my son, Justice, with an angel of our own to watch over him.*

Are They Your Stepchildren?

I glanced sharply at my husband's uncle to see if he was kidding. His benign expression clearly told me otherwise.

"Nope," I answered. "I'm their birth mother."

Now it was Uncle Jack's turn to be shocked.

I felt around on my nose. No telltale evil-stepmother wart. I have the vertical classical C-section scar to prove that I had shared my umbilical cord at one time or another with all four of my children, but I wasn't exactly keen about rolling up my shirt for Exhibit A.

I was mildly amused, yet puzzled over his question. Why on earth did he pose such a question?

We were into the second day of our visit in the home of my husband's aunt and uncle who lived in a quaint town two hours north of us. We had promised for ages we would come and visit, and finally we made good on our promise. Our boys explored their acreage for adventure and fished in their pond. Our baby daughter snuggled in her granddad's lap. While relatives buzzed with news and cooking, Uncle Jack was out in the breezeway, chain-smoking with his ever-present grin.

I inventoried the events from the day before. We had arrived in a van filled with kids and in-laws, suitcases and gifts. We had thrown a surprise celebration in honor of my father-in-law's eightieth birthday, complete with balloons, potluck cuisine, and a huge birthday cake.

Then it dawned on me. I could see it all from Uncle Jack's vantage point.

My husband, Stephen, had been tending to the kids most of our visit there, filling their plates, changing the baby's diaper, putting her down for a nap, disciplining the boys when it was called for.

What was natural to us—Stephen's hands-on approach to the kids—must've struck Uncle Jack as rather odd. After all, his was a generation mainly raised by mothers, not fathers. Stephen's role as a househubby had transferred itself into everyday living, even down to a family gathering such as this.

Stephen and I often compared our roles with what was traditional in the 1950s.

I now understand a man's attitude at the end of a long, mind-draining day at the office, followed by a forty-minute tangle with rush-hour traffic. I know, I know, you're probably thinking I come home to chilled martinis, pressed newspapers, and those pink feathery slippers. But that's not all that my husband wears.

Stephen now understands a stay-at-home mother's attitude at the end of a long day. He wants a real conversation with a grown-up other than "I'm not telling you again! Quit eating dirt!"

Working a full-time career outside the home made me lose sight of minor details, like the birth order of our kids. Stephen knew all the words to the Barney song, their favorite hiding places, and the perfect antidote to rainy-day blues (playing pirates with Dad on a pile of cushions, blankets, and pillows).

The height of my cooking involved mixing sliced hot dogs with macaroni and cheese, while Stephen's cooking would have Julia Childs begging for his culinary secrets (what zest a teaspoon of peanut butter brings to spaghetti sauce!).

While I fought deadlines, Stephen fought clotheslines. He clutched his chest one day when he saw me toss underwear into the washing machine along with bath towels. Imagine my chagrin. Up until then, I didn't know I was laundry challenged.

As a working mom, much like the working fathers of the Greatest Generation, I also lost sight of major details. I missed my kids' first toddling steps, first loose tooth, and other heart-tugging milestones.

I would be curious to know if, back in the 1950s, anyone asked a father, "Are they your stepchildren?"

Stephen called me the other day at work, whispering, "You've gotta listen to this. Madison is singing in her crib."

I sat at my desk with its typical clutter of pens, steno notebooks, bottled water, a mess of flowcharts and phone messages, and my family smiling at me from several framed pictures. As Stephen held the phone over the crib, I swiveled away from the watchful glow of my computer monitor. Tears welled up in my eyes as my beautiful baby girl serenaded me.

The times, Uncle Jack, they are a-changing.

Jennifer Oliver

"Honey, I've gotta work late.
Can you swing by and pick up the kids?"

A Mom for Working Moms

For over fifteen years, I stayed home while other women came in and out my door on their way to work. In a hurried morning haste, they handed me diaper bags, jackets, and their most precious treasures—their children. For over fifteen years, I felt each mother's struggle as she left her kids to go to the office. Because at one time I also had left my kids in day care to go to work, I knew their guilt and apprehension. My hope was to become their most valuable partner in parenting—their "co-mom"!

I had four kids of my own. My husband, Steve, was unable to work due to a serious illness. I needed to support my family while taking care of my kids and my husband. Licensed family home day care was the perfect fit for us! Even though it was our livelihood, we thought of it as a ministry. We could provide a loving family environment while moms worked. It was a chance to share God's love on a daily basis with kids and their families. Besides that, I could be there for my own children all day long, and my children had built-in playmates to grow up with!

Even with my husband's illness, he got involved in the kids' lives. Steve played his guitar and sang for them, or sat at the table to eat with them. It helped him have purpose and meaning in his life. When the parents came at the end of the day, they often spilled their hearts out to Steve or me. We became part of their extended family. Our home seemed like their home.

Even our teens got in on the act. My daughter planned preschool lessons. She took the kids on "alphabet walks" to look for things that began with different letters. My teen son showed the boys how to shoot basketball. As our kids grew older, they learned that younger kids were looking to them as role models. They knew there was a responsibility that went with that.

Of course, not everything was easy. Our house couldn't stay as neat and organized as I wanted. There was a certain lack of privacy having people in and out all the time, including day-care inspectors! Things got broken or torn up at times. If one kid got sick, several more followed. There were occasional misunderstandings that had to be worked through. Our kids had to share more than the average child. As they got older, their rooms became off-limits to ensure a certain amount of privacy.

Because our day care was a home setting, it was less formal than a huge day-care center. We provided a mixture of structure and free time so the kids could just be kids. The boys would pull out the box of old fatigues from the Army surplus store and head to the backyard to play army for hours. The girls would make beautiful necklaces from big wooden beads or make a store for Barbie to shop in. On rainy days, tents made from sheets and blankets covered a whole room.

We went to the zoo or had picnics at the park. I took the younger ones to watch the older kids in a play at school. I read Bible stories before nap time. Then older kids had quiet reading time or played outside. There were swimming lessons, vacation Bible school, and weekly trips to the library to check out books. The older kids gained confidence reading to the younger ones.

Because I knew it was important for moms to know what their kids did during the day, I made a newsletter that had a chart of planned meals, snacks, and activities for the week. To include the moms, I asked for certain supplies, such as empty liter pop bottles for crafts. At pick-up time, I always tried to report some cute things the kids did or any problems we needed to work on together. It was important to make sure the moms knew that I was there to help them rear their kids, not rear them myself.

There were some scary moments, like the time a drunk driver rear-ended our van as we came back from a trip to the park. Fortunately, we had just practiced our safety drills the day before and everyone was wearing seat belts. No one was hurt, just shook-up! Another time I dreaded calling a parent at work. It was the first day of afternoon kindergarten for one of the boys. His mom had paid to have his hair stylishly cut. Just before lunch, he came out of the other room with scissors. He had cut a huge bald spot right in the front of his head! Or how about the time the little girl asked me why I didn't have a job. I thought, *I sure am working hard for someone who has no job!*

We also had sad times. My husband died at the young age of thirty-seven. Not only was I brokenhearted, but also I had to help my own kids and all the day-care kids through their grief. Steve had been like a second dad to them. Of course, I had to keep on working. We gave one another lots of hugs!

One day I started crying as we drove to the park. One of the kids asked me if I was okay. I told her I missed Steve. She said, "I do, too." Before I knew it, a whole van of kids started chanting, "We miss Steve! We miss Steve!" Needless to say, I had to pull over to regain my composure.

I'm still very close to most of the families. Last Mother's Day I got a card from a mom of a twenty-year-old, with a copy of a card her son made for her while in my care. She thanked me for being a mom for her when she was at work!

Eva Juliuson

Angels in Seminole

In July 2002, Deborah woke up to three very hungry young children with just $2.23 in her purse. The night before, her husband had left her and the children, swearing that he would never return. The children, two boys and a girl, were ages four, two, and five months, respectively.

Even before he left, the children's father—and her husband—was seldom home. When he was at home, they feared his presence. As soon as they heard his voice, the two boys would run and hide under their beds. The infant girl cried unceasingly.

When her husband finally decided never to return, she and her children would no longer be subjected to abuse; however, now there would be nothing with which to feed, clothe, and shelter her children. She would have to replace what little income he had brought in. As she picked up the clothes her husband had left in the house, a $20 bill fell out of a shirt pocket. Deborah's first thought was to buy food for her children.

Deborah fed her children egg sandwiches, then they bathed, put on their best clean clothing, climbed into her old rusty 1979 Dodge and drove through Seminole, Oklahoma, to look for a job. Deborah and her children went to every plant, restaurant, and department store in the small town but found nothing. The children got in and out of the car along with their mother so that by noon they were very tired and stressed. As her children cried for something to eat, Deborah prayed to God for guidance and the strength to help her get a job to support her family.

The one place she had forgotten to try was the local Sonic restaurant. The manager was an older Native American woman. Grandma Harjo, as she was called by those who knew her, needed someone to work the 4:00 PM to 11:00 PM shift. She offered Deborah a starting hourly wage of $5.50. She also indicated that Deborah could start that night if she wished to do so.

Excited, Deborah fed her children and herself at the Sonic, then raced to get ready for her first job since high school. Deborah drove to a nearby lifelong friend's home to see if her friend's teenage daughter would babysit her three children. The fourteen-year-old girl agreed. That evening, Deborah and her children knelt down in thanksgiving to God for what she had received that day.

The weeks passed and summer changed to fall, then winter. The heating bills added a strain to an already stretched income. The old Dodge needed tires, antifreeze, and an oil change. One day, exhausted from the pressure of work and concerns for her old vehicle and the welfare of her children, Deborah unlocked her car door. Inside she found four brand-new tires in the back seat and a gray envelope with enough money to winterize her car. Amazed, Deborah could not believe her good fortune, but there was no note—nothing to identify her benefactor.

Deborah went to an auto repair garage, where she gave the owner what money she had and offered to clean his office in exchange for mounting and balancing her tires and winterizing her car.

After nearly six months at Sonic, Deborah was working six days a week instead of five, yet there still was not enough money. Christmas was just around the corner. One of her fellow employees told her that Saint Benedict's Catholic Church in Shawnee gave food and Christmas gifts to struggling families.

Deborah made the seventeen-mile drive to Shawnee, where Father Maurus, pastor of Saint Benedict, greeted her and provided clothing, food, and toys for her children. Pleased, she thanked God and quickly returned to Seminole. Now she had the problem of hiding the gifts from her children because it was still a few days before Christmas.

On Christmas Eve, some of Sonic's usual customers came to celebrate the holiday before the restaurant closed for Christmas. People Deborah had known all of her life ordered a variety of food. After she served them and they paid, they gave her their change as Christmas gifts. Among the customers were Father Basil Keenan, pastor of Immaculate Conception Church of Seminole, members from other local churches, people from the Seminole American Legion, and employees from Seminole State College. They were all there.

As usual, Deborah was ready to leave the restaurant near midnight. She was very tired having served so many people that Christmas Eve. She hoped she would have enough strength to put up a Christmas tree and move the presents she had received from Saint Benedict's church up from the basement to her small living room.

It was very dark when the business lights were turned off. Deborah walked to her car, and as soon as she opened the door, a neatly wrapped box fell out, hitting her right foot. Now, wide-awake, she could see that her rusty old 1979 Dodge was full from top to bottom with boxes of all shapes and sizes. She turned on the car's interior light and found blue jeans, shirts, shoes, and underclothing for little boys and girls. A note asked her to check the trunk. Slowly getting out of her car, she walked back to the trunk and opened it. In the trunk were boxes filled with food, including a large ham, canned goods, bread, fresh vegetables, Christmas candy, pies, cakes, fruitcakes, and more. Enough, it seemed, for a month. Stunned, her eyes filled with tears. As she drove the five miles to her house, she said a prayer of thanksgiving to God for the kindness of friends and strangers.

As she watched the sun rise in the eastern Oklahoma sky on Christmas morning and heard the laughter of her three children, Deborah Meeks treasured always in her heart and mind the people in the small town of Seminole, Oklahoma. Yes, Deborah would go on to say there are angels, and they live in Seminole, Oklahoma, U.S.A!

Stephen A. Peterson

Being a Working Mom

Being a working mom was one thing, but being a divorced working mom, especially in the 1960s when "divorce" was a very dirty word, was something else again. Some days I wondered why I bothered, days when I wasn't sure I could cope for another hour.

And then there was Christmas. A time I had always cherished. A time I had tried to keep free of commercialism. A time I loved deeply. But that year it was a time of despair and frustration. The kids would receive gifts, of course; my sisters would send them lots, and I was sure I could fill their stockings with little puzzles and things from one of the cheaper stores, but there would be no Christmas cheer: no tree, no "extras," no turkey dinner. And after living on baked beans on toast and macaroni and cheese week after week, I couldn't bear the thought of my little ones being without even a Christmas cracker.

I worked for a small company, and the office manager asked if I would play the piano at the children's Christmas party. I said I would, and she told me that the names of all the children in attendance were put into a hat and whoever's name was drawn received the tree with all its decorations. She also said that there was a man in the plant who had ten children, and he always won, so I shouldn't get my hopes up.

I had almost forgotten what hope was.

At the party, I looked at the tree sparkling with tinsel and bells, and I felt a deep and sad longing. Not just for the tree itself, but for all that the tree represented: the essence of Christmas, the carols, the joy. I watched as the children played games and sat shyly on Santa's knee to tell him their secret longings. Oh, how I wished there really was a Santa Claus.

Then came the cake and ice cream, the carol singing, and the candy canes. I thought, *Well, even if we don't have anything at home, they have had a good day today.* I was so glad for that little company I worked with.

At last it was time to go home, and after helping with the cleanup, the office manager announced that it was time for the drawing. I pretended to be busy wiping down the tables so that no one would see the tears of disappointment I knew would come. Then I heard, "And the winner is—Michael Clifton!"

What? I couldn't believe it! My son had won the tree! The sales manager brought the tree to our basement apartment, and the joy on my children's faces was almost more than I could bear. I said a silent prayer of thanks, but there was more to come. The general manager of the company gave me a turkey. The office manager gave me a Christmas cake. The sales manager gave me a bottle of wine.

Such bounty. I was overcome with gratitude. And we had a wonderful Christmas.

It was much, much later that I found out that Michael's was the only name that had been put in the hat!

Dorothy Megan Clifton

Waving the White Flag

I have found that the best way to give advice to your children is to find out what they want and then advise them to do it.

Harry S. Truman

It had been one of those days. First, I lost the freelance job that would have supported me for the next two months. Then, I discovered I needed outpatient surgery, only minimally covered by my insurance. Next, a torrential downpour turned my basement furniture into islands. Instead of spending the evening creating a stunning new resume, I was duct taping trash sacks to the dribbling basement walls and sopping up puddles with towels. I started upstairs to search for more trash sacks and tripped over a stray board left by the rascals who waterproofed my basement! I picked up the board and was instantly stabbed with a splinter. I stomped up the stairs.

"I give up," I said to the dirty dishes in the kitchen sink. "I can't take anymore," I said to the pile of unopened bills cluttering the kitchen table. I shook the white towel and water flew across the countertops. Then I remembered the old Westerns, when the bullet-riddled good guys tied a handkerchief on a rifle butt and waved it at the enemy just to get a moment's respite.

It was time for me to officially throw in my towel.

I went outside and tied the towel to a board. I walked into the yard and waved my flag at the sky, and said, "I surrender." It was a good thing, too, because I suddenly realized I was ankle deep in water. And I was wearing my good shoes. I leaned the flag against the porch and dragged myself up to bed.

The next morning, the beat-up-looking flag made me smile. I felt better now that I had officially let go of control. I believed in the idea of an abundant and beneficent universe; I believed that I did not have to struggle so mightily to get what I needed. But I hadn't been able to really incorporate such serenity into my everyday life. Maybe this flag was a first step.

Every time I came in and out of the house, I saw the flag. Despite that constant reminder, I still struggled. Sure, my basement dried up, and, yes, I got a new client. But I felt "on the edge" rather than brimming with abundance. I saw various friends being rewarded for their persistence and faith, and I knew I wouldn't be so lucky.

"What is that rag and board on our porch?" my daughter Sarah asked.

"My white flag," I told her. "I am practicing surrender."

Meanwhile, I began noticing other people's flags: colorful cardinals on a quilted field of leaves; a sassy black cat, jauntily swinging from a porch pole; a winsome dog wagging his tale. These flags were crisp and lovely, flying proudly from well-turned poles. Suddenly, my flag looked old and tattered. My flag had been thrown together in desperation. Now I wanted a white flag that was an act of deliberation.

"Will you make a white flag for me for my birthday?" I asked Sarah.

"What kind?" she asked.

"Big enough to be noticed on the porch. Sturdy enough to be outside. You can choose how it looks."

As soon as I spoke those words, I worried, *What if I don't like the way the flag looks? What if it simply isn't what I envisioned? What if it's too large or too small?* Then I had to laugh at myself: I wanted control over everything, even the shape of my surrender!

The morning of my birthday, Sarah put a long pole in my hands. It was spray-painted gold, with an elegant carved top, and held a beautifully proportioned, dazzling white flag. The flag was aesthetic, dramatic, and elegant. Slowly I walked outside and hung the flag near my porch light, where it was fully visible yet sheltered from the rain. The flag tilted a little to the right. I climbed onto a chair to straighten it, and by the time I climbed down, it tilted again. I tried again, perfect, and yet, the moment I stepped off the chair, the flag became askew.

Then I realized, the flag was already working, reminding me to flow with imperfection, to enjoy what was offered. I saluted my crooked flag and went inside to make a birthday wish.

Deborah Shouse

To Toast a Dad

It was an incident Terry could not appreciate or even fully understand: he needed cookies for his first grade class. The day I found out was the day before the cookies were to be consumed by forty-something six-year-olds. The note, sent a week earlier, had been folded and left in a book.

"Terry! This says you need cookies tomorrow!"

"Yeah, Mom, chocolate chip, sugar cookies, and peanut butter. I told the teacher you would bake them."

It wouldn't have been such a big deal, but we lived a good twenty minutes from town, and our second son was just a few months old. I was working the midnight shift at a telephone answering service and had just gone back to work that very week. So I was a little more tired than usual trying to get used to the hours.

Gil, my husband, worked day shift, and I slept after he came home. Sometimes I was lucky enough to get a nap with the baby, but not today; I had cookies to bake. To top it off, we used propane and bought it about every six weeks in 100-gallon bottles. Instantly, I hoped there was enough gas.

Nowadays children take store-bought cookies for safety reasons, but back then no mother was going to send any less than homemade cookies from scratch. I was no different.

Once Terry was off to school, I immediately started baking. Sometime before lunch, I ran out of gas. Not a "big" problem because Gil's mom lived next door. I quickly called her, and, of course, she said bring the baby first then return with the ingredients.

So back and forth I ran with cookie sheets, flour, sugar, and cooling racks. I was still baking when Terry came in from school, so I left the last of the cookies cooling and had "Meemaw" put them in the carrying containers—a double-pie holder and a large square cake holder, both Tupperware with easy-tote handles.

Right before Gil got home from work, I told Terry to run and get the two containers of cookies from Meemaw's. I was ready to drop, and the baby was awake, I had supper to make, and where was Terry? He should be back!

I stuck my head out the door just in time to see a little freckle-faced boy with a mass of red curly hair singing and swinging both containers of cookies. One of his hands swinging one way, while the other was swinging in the opposite direction. And he was skipping!

My yell echoed across the yard just as the lids flew off both containers. Cookies flew through the air onto half-thawed ground. I could hear Terry saying how sorry he was, somewhere behind my tears. He was trying to pick them up, and just as I got to him, I saw that he was crying, too.

"It's okay, you can't save them, honey. They are dirty, and my little boy's class isn't eating dirty cookies."

We walked back to the house, both feeling sorry for ourselves.

When Gil came in, he saw the shape I was in. "I will go to town and buy some cookies," he suggested, knowing I would pull a no-sleep-before-midnight shift.

"No. Terry is not taking store-bought cookies to school," I said.

"I will call his teacher and tell her he cannot bring them, and that's that."

I don't remember what happened later that night; but I was one depressed momma. I never called the teacher; I thought I'd just send a note the next morning. Around midnight I went to work.

The next morning when I got home, there on the kitchen table were the two containers "magically" filled with cookies. Gil had left for work; Meemaw was with the boys.

"Meemaw, you shouldn't have made these cookies! It was too much work so late at night."

"I didn't make those cookies," she said, about the same time it dawned on me that she had no idea what had happened.

"These are the cookies you made, aren't they?" she asked.

"No, and I don't know where they came from if you didn't bake them."

Nevertheless, my son left for school with his cookies, all three flavors.

That night when Gil came in from work, I realized what kind of man I had married and exactly what kind of father our boys were lucky enough to have.

When I asked him where the cookies had come from, he said he baked them.

"You've never baked a cookie in your life!"

"No, but you have recipes," he said. "I can read a recipe."

"But, Gil, we had no gas. The stove wouldn't work, and your mom didn't even know Terry spilled the cookies! How did you do this?"

"I baked them in the toaster oven," he said.

"I baked them three at a time," he said through a grin—and it had taken him only all night long.

Jo Ann Holbrook

Relearning How to Say Good-bye

When we got into her room, Natasha smiled as the other chattering children gathered around her. She barely noticed when I kissed her good-bye. I was relieved at how easy it had been for her to part from me. I, on the other hand, was teary; my chest ached. I was thankful it had been this easy. When I came to pick her up eight hours later, she ran to me, tugging on my clothes as she tried to clamber up into my arms. We held each other joyfully, as though we had not been together for months.

On the second day, however, Natasha waved good-bye to her brother, Alister, and started babbling with less enthusiasm than usual as she watched where we were going. When she saw the green restaurant awning, she gasped. She saw the round bagel sign on her right and stared at me.

"Mama. Mama." At the fire station, she burst into tears. "Mama, no. Mama, no." As I turned up the hill, she uttered a final plea. "Please, Mama, no."

Three little words, each one more hopeless than the last. I glanced back to see tears trickling from her large brown eyes, down her pinkish cheeks. Tears began to stream from my eyes. When we stopped, we cried as I took her from the car, and we held each other.

"I'm so sorry, baby girl," I said as she held on to my shoulders, wrapping her clinging, little fists in my hair. "It's going to be okay," I told her, wanting to believe it myself.

The caregiver took Tashi from my arms. Her face was red, her voice high and loud as she cried from fear and anger. "I'll see you soon." I kissed her quickly and walked away, still hearing her cry, while I stifled my own tears.

I dabbed at my mascara and showed up at work every day for over two weeks with puffy red eyes, smudged eyeliner, a pink nose, and heavy heart. Natasha and I repeated this ritual of grieving separation daily. One morning Rashida, my coworker, brought me a cup of tea and put her arm around me. "It's hard for you to leave your baby, but everything will be okay," she said. "You can't only tell Natasha this, but you must believe it yourself."

The next day, before I dropped Natasha off, I said to her: "I'm going to take Alister to day care and Tashi to work, then I am going to school."

"Mama," Alister said, and laughed, "you mean, you are going to take *me* to school and Tashi to day care and then *you* go to work."

"Oh, I'm taking *you* to work and Tashi to school, and then I am going to day care." Alister let out a squeal and set about correcting me again. We repeated this a couple more times, and Natasha started to laugh.

After we dropped off Alister, I said, "Okay, Tashi, now where am I going to take you? Work?"

"No, Mama. I go to day care." She smiled and we played the mixed-up destination game a little more.

Natasha's lip started quivering when she saw the large bagel hovering ahead.

"I love you, baby girl. Will you show me your pictures when I pick you up?"

"No, Mama. I want to stay with you."

"I want to stay with you, too, but I have to go to work. We will be together soon." There was silence as we passed the fire station. I waited for a sign of peace from Natasha.

"I'm going to play in the sprinklers today." This time Natasha didn't look at me with big glistening eyes. Instead, she looked out of the window with brighter eyes and waved. "Miss Lucy! Miss Lucy!"

When I took Natasha out of the car, she held tightly to me. "Mama, Mama."

I felt her quivering breath as she released me. Tears rolled down from our eyes as we looked at each other, but the anxiety and fear were gone.

"It's okay to be sad. But it's good to be happy, too. I love you, baby girl."

"I love you too, Mama."

I still had to fix my makeup when I got to work, but this time my heart was intact. I brought Rashida a cup of tea and gave her a big hug.

Maya Fleischmann

A Simple Recipe

As I pulled the pan out of the oven, my son glanced at the meat. "Chicken again?" he asked.

"I thought you liked this recipe." The chicken dish was easy to make. It assembled in five minutes and cooked for an hour.

"Don't we eat this once a week?"

I sighed. Working night shift, I slept days. I understood that my children did not realize I ate dinner with them when what I would have preferred was breakfast—an omelet, pancakes, or a quick bowl of oatmeal. The simplest thing for me to do after I woke up was to put something in the oven, shower, and dress for work before eating dinner as a family. As I chewed my chicken, I knew I needed a way to resolve the issue. During work that night, I devised a plan.

The next day I introduced my proposal. After I passed the meat loaf and side dishes, I reached for my secret weapon. I placed my old cookbook on the table, shifted in my seat, and announced, "I made a decision." Looking at my son and daughter, I said, "You will each pick a recipe before I go grocery shopping. Once a week, you will prepare dinner after school. You are both in high school, old enough to cook."

"Anything we want?" My daughter was not a fan of meatloaf.

I nodded. "Whatever you want; just remember you make it for dinner." I was not sure they understood that work was involved.

With interest, my daughter started to page through the book. "What about this chicken tetrazzini?"

I glanced at the ingredients. It was something I never would have made for my children because of the sherry and whipping cream in the recipe. Afraid they would smell something different, I tended to cook as I had for years, without creams or a variety of spices. "It sounds good." I took the book and handed it across the table to my son. While eating his dinner, he paged through the recipes. I relished the lack of complaints. But I wondered if their initial interest actually would transition into cooking the food.

As weeks progressed, both of them picked only new recipes. We started to eat differently. They served me dishes I would not have attempted to serve them. It made me regret not having initiated a cooking chore sooner. I always asked for other help around the house, mainly in the cleaning department.

Months later, my children were still cooking. Perhaps not every week, as I initially expected, but their behavior toward food changed. Over time they learned differences in recipes, how extensive ingredient lists could result in time investments. As they shopped at the grocery store, they began to understand the cost of food as well.

Then my son began to bake the chocolate chip cookies he enjoyed eating. Soon he claimed he could make them better than I could. Why would I even try to compete? He was taking care of one of his needs.

Although we still ate dinner instead of breakfast before I left for work, the partial transfer of responsibility for cooking to my children was a fulfilling decision. It gave them a sense of control over their lives. It was one of the best parenting plans I ever devised. It was a simple recipe with all the right ingredients.

Linda Hanson

Mom-entum

The prospect of returning to work after Erin was born was nauseating. I approached my employer about a job-share arrangement and found that it was a fairly new policy and not very user-friendly. I soon located a job share in my field with a different employer. It was a fifteen-minute commute down country roads and a satisfying job (with a little promotion to boot!). Then I was on the hunt for a caregiver.

My mother had been a stay-at-home mom and so had her mother. My older sister had been able to stay at home, and when her kids got older, she worked from home. My auntie had stayed home, too. These women, the role models in my life, all very much wanted for me to be able to stay home with my kids. All were excited that if I had to go back to work, at least I was able to work only half-time. None of them had really walked in my shoes.

For the first time, I had no role models. None of them had ever had to recruit and hire a caregiver—someone so vital to the family, who would care for our babies many days per week, who would teach and nurture them, who would be a part of their upbringing and their memories.

We lucked out. Through word of mouth from a former

colleague, we found a fabulous lady with home day care who was on the bus route and had her own young children. For a year and a half, I worked this ideal job-share arrangement: Thursday and Friday one week, Monday through Wednesday the next, followed by one whole week off with the kids. Boardroom one day, playgroup the next. A dream come true.

Then, as the reality of today's world goes, there were layoffs (luckily, my position went unscathed), but a few months later, my job-share partner resigned. Loving my job and wanting to plan ahead for uncertain times, I decided to apply for the other half of my job and return to work full time.

It's been three months since I took on the full-time role. Things are going well, but I am still walking a tightrope some days, trying to find "the balance." My husband has been most supportive, allowing me to make my own decisions, alleviating the "bad mother" guilt at all the right times. I am trying to keep my work life out of family time, but sometimes home life creeps into work. I guess that's because my job is only something I do, but being a mom is part of who I am. I think that brings a lot to my job.

I love my two kids more than anything. I have been a working mom, a stay-at-home mom, and a hybrid of the two—none of which have made me any less of a mother to them.

If ever I could be a role model to working moms, I would tell them these things:

1. A great caregiver is paramount. You need someone who feels like extended family, someplace where you know your kids will be listened to and loved, a situation in which after a while you don't feel the need to call several times a day to check in.
2. Job shares are terrific! They are a great way to ease back to work, if you can manage one.

3. A supportive spouse is a must—you are a team! A spouse can reassure you, alleviate the guilt, and do the laundry!

4. Balance is key; as much as possible, leave the work at work. When you are at home, give the family (yourself included) your full attention, and take from them enough to fill your heart every day. Read books, work outside together, play, snuggle lots.

The word "momentum" has "mom" at the start for a reason! We are constantly in motion no matter what hat we're wearing—and we should be able to love every minute of it!

Jennifer Nicholson

5

SUPERWOMAN— JUGGLING IT ALL

Women are like tea bags, they don't know how strong they are until they get into hot water.

Eleanor Roosevelt

"Hey, Honey . . . did you get the promotion?"

The Breast Pump

*Divide your movements into easy-to-do sections.
If you fail, divide again.*

Peter Nivio Zarlenga

When my wife started back to work after the birth of our son, we had agreed that continuing him on breast milk would be the best thing to do.

We went to the store and bought the deluxe breast pump. We purchased insulator bags for the bottles. We cleared out extra space in the refrigerator.

Then six hours into the first day, my wife called me at work.

"Ken, I can't bear it anymore."

"Your job?" I asked.

"No, this breast pump," she complained. "I feel like a cow in the big city."

"In the city?"

"Well, actually in the toilet stall, where I just sat milking away my entire lunch break while listening to the young secretaries gossip over the noise of the hand blower."

"You sit on the toilet?"

"Well, where did you think I would do it?" she asked. "In the copier room? What would I say? 'Come on in, guys, don't mind me; I'm just sucking nourishment from my breast. Oh, and by the way, the legal size paper's over there on the table, under my blouse.'"

That night we regrouped. We reminded ourselves of the health benefits of breast milk, and my wife reconfirmed her desire to put her best foot forward.

Noon the next day she called.

"I feel like I'm doing something illegal," she announced.

"Why?"

"Because I hide out in the bathroom."

"People don't care," I said. "I'm sure everyone supports your decision."

"What do you suppose people who don't know what I am doing in there think when they walk into the bathroom and all they hear is the low hum of an electrical device behind a bathroom stall?"

"Maybe your boss should provide a breast pumping room," I suggested. "Where the new mothers can . . ."

"Sit around watching each other pump their bare breasts?" she interrupted.

"Well . . ."

"Maybe we could also share home remedies for chapped nipples," she added sarcastically. "We could even take turns bringing snacks."

On the second night, we held hands and prayed to God. Still, my wife assured me, she was dedicated to breast milk.

Come the third day, she was on the phone by 10 AM.

"There is only one stall close to the outlet to plug in my pump," she explained.

"So?"

"So, I had to wait until the stall was free, which wasn't easy when my breasts were so engorged they began erupting. I had to open my bra and empty out on the floor."

"That's embarrassing," I said.

"Actually, the bad part is when the milk ran down around the feet of whoever was on the inside of the stall I needed. I imagine she'll throw away her shoes after something like that."

When I got home, I noticed the deluxe breast pump and insulator bags were stuffed into the trash can.

I never said a word.

Ken Swarner

Interview

Hundreds of thousands of us will change jobs this year. We will give ourselves a pep talk, struggle with updating our resumés trying to put our skills and accomplishments in the best light without embellishing, schedule appointments, and figure out what to wear.

Then comes the day of reckoning, what we have been looking forward to and dreading: the interview. The interview process may be broken down in to several component stages. There is the initial euphoria: "Queen of the Known Universe? That is the perfect job for me!"

As the interview date approaches, so do the jitters. One minute you are just fine, and the next minute all the extra blood in your body rushes to your stomach, your hands develop a tremor, your eyes start to water, your mouth dries up, and you find yourself shouting at your family, "What do you mean what time is supper? I am practicing shaking hands right now! Clasp, pump, pump, release."

And then comes the day of the interview. You may have noticed, as I sometimes have, that God in his heaven has a kind of funny sense of humor. Not always funny "ha-ha." You may rest assured that the day of the interview will be the day that your watch stops, the toilet clogs and over-

flows, the cat develops grand mal seizures, your carbure-
tor goes out, and you find that your three pairs of brand-
new pantyhose have been made into the World's Most
Powerful Slingshot by your precious little feller. This will
throw your whole schedule into disarray. (Please note that
it is nearly impossible to put pantyhose on in a car.)

You are not a child. As a friend of mine once said, "You
have been to two cow ropings and a county fair." You have
made allowances for the quirks of the universe in your
schedule. You arrive for your interview. You are not late. In
fact, you are early. Forty-five minutes early. No, thanks,
you don't need a magazine. You will just sit quietly and
compose yourself. For forty-five minutes. While at home
the toilet you thought you did not have time to deal with
continues to cheerily gurgle on and on and on.

"Ms. Jones?"

You have been sucking on your tongue for forty-five
minutes, with your hands splayed out on your thighs in
the hope that they will be neither sweaty nor cold. This
was wasted effort. As you stand to meet your prospective
employer, perspiration gushes from every pore in your
body. You reach out to shake hands, thinking, *Clasp, pump,
pump, release. Wait! Man! Did I just say pump, pump out loud?*
You gasp in dismay. And aspirate your chewing gum. That
is okay, because you are not supposed to be chewing gum
anyway, and although you meant to swallow it when your
name was called, at least it is gone. But now you can't get
a breath and your vision is dimming.

As soon as the helpful receptionist has Heimliched you
and given you a glass of water, you are ready for your
interview to continue, and you can feel assured that you
will be remembered.

Your interviewer knows that you are nervous and
wants to make you feel at ease. She may give you a brief
overview of the organization and the job to give you time

to settle yourself. She may ask you how this sounds to you. Save your so-called humor for some other time. Do not mention anything about work-release programs. Remember, she does not know you and may not know when you are kidding.

As the interview progresses, you may find yourself experiencing a moment of calm. You know who you are, what your abilities are. This sense of calm is a great relief for a moment or two. You may feel that you and the interviewer are on common ground and that you are responding in an intelligent and professional way. But there is an aftermath to the huge tsunami of adrenaline you have been surfing since you woke up this morning. And that aftermath is the dreaded yawn. Pinch yourself, imagine disaster, pretend there is a spider in your shoe. Do whatever you must do, but do not yawn. Don't. Do. *Yaaaa-haaa-haaaa.* It.

Also, do not mention clogging. I mean, if you clog dance and you love it, you may mention it. But suppose you are nervous and when she asks you to tell her a little about yourself, your mind suddenly becomes a big Mojave Desert of anything interesting. Try not to grasp desperately at the first irrational straw that comes to you. Especially if it is clog dancing. And isn't it interesting, from a psychological standpoint, that the first thing that pops into your mind is clogging? Something you know absolutely nothing about. Interesting in a horrible, horrible way. Interesting in a way that you are bound to spend many, many sleepless nights considering.

Elizabeth Bussey Sowdal

The Ideal Situation

When I tell another mother that I work from home, and she says, "Oh, that must be the ideal situation," I know one thing about her, even if we've never met before. She does not now, nor has she ever, worked from home.

She has never rushed to the post office to mail a manuscript while still covered in toddler vomit (FYI, there *is* a way to make those lines move more quickly).

She has never had an important phone interview with a well-known politician interrupted by her daughter screaming, "Mommy, come quick, James is peeing on the dog's head!" Dogs drink from the toilet, and little boys can't wait, no matter what's in the way.

When I left my full-time newspaper reporting job to have my first child nearly fourteen years ago, I pictured myself, after a suitable recovery and bonding period of, say, a week, churning out journalistic masterpieces on my computer while my daughter burbled contentedly in her swing.

I'll never forget the look on our Lifestyle editor's face when I popped into his office to tell him I'd be ready for some freelance work in a couple of weeks. "I'll tell you what," said the wise father of three, "you call me."

I never did. My son, James, arrived twenty-one months after my daughter, Elizabeth, so for the next four years I'm not sure I called anyone other than my pediatrician, my mother, and the local Chinese take-out joint.

But once I was able to shower regularly and think (fairly) clearly again, I decided to resume my writing career—working from home, of course, because it's the ideal situation.

First, I set up a real office. Okay, it was (and still is) the spare room, and my desk was wedged between the stepladder and the vacuum, sort of behind the bassinette and boxes of maternity and baby clothes that never seemed to make it into the attic. But from this impressive nerve center I planned, yet once more, to churn out journalistic masterpieces as my two perfectly behaved toddlers played contentedly nearby.

Except, having not signed on to my grand plan, my kids yelled, hit, and bit each other, fell, and threw up, creating a work environment that made my former newsroom, with its blaring police radios, televisions, and cursing reporters, seem as tranquil as a New Age yoga class. And that was during the three days a week the sitter was around to help.

Even if I could have ignored the kicking and screaming, try focusing on a deadline when someone slips a little hand in yours and wants you, not the sitter, not Daddy, not even Barney, to come collect leaves, have a tea party, or wash and buff Matchbox cars.

I always opted for the tea party because I knew that in a few years my babies would be in school, and I'd have all the time in the world to churn out journalistic masterpieces while, under the supervision of their teachers, they evolved into prodigies.

However, on my daughter's first day of kindergarten, I signed up to help with the class holiday party. Being a new parent, I was unaware that a school sign-up sheet is the equivalent to one of those "sell your soul" contracts. Before I knew it, I was a field-trip chaperone, library volunteer, Brownie leader, Spring Festival clean-up committee chair, and the mother of them all, Room Parent. Soon, I was spending more time at school than my children were.

Occasionally, I would feebly try to explain that, yes, I was "at home," and therefore, "available" at all hours, but I also "worked," and therefore, I was not available at all hours. This was met with a suspicious stare, as if I was trying to concoct a bogus alibi that would allow me to shirk cupcake-baking duty.

When I missed an important deadline because I had to decorate the school gym with cornstalks and pumpkins for the fifth grade Halloween party (how time flies when you're on committees!), I tried to take comfort in the fact that my children appreciated having an involved parent. Later that day, my daughter informed me that my presence at so many school events was becoming embarrassing.

When my children were a little older, I also tried to squeeze in some afternoon working hours, figuring they could do homework or relax quietly while I churned out those journalistic masterpieces. This worked so beautifully that often there were periods of up to five whole minutes when I didn't have to define a word, help glue together a shoebox diorama, assist with a math problem, or break up an argument.

Of course, at times I laid down the law. Once, when I absolutely had to finish an article that day, I told my kids, "Don't you dare knock on my office door unless the house catches fire—and I'm not making rice, so that's not going to happen." My children call my most frequently incinerated side dish "deadline rice."

The moment I went into my office, the washer began to

leak. Soon there was an inch of water on the kitchen floor. Then two. As the tide rose, according to my kids, the conversation went like this:

Elizabeth: I think we should get Mom!

James: I don't know. She said "fire" not "water." And she looked pretty mad.

Elizabeth: I think flood counts the same as fire. It says so in the Bible.

Yes, they got me, and the house, if not the deadline, was saved.

So you must be thinking after all this grousing that I've abandoned working at home for a safe and sane job in an office uncluttered by laundry, where I'm safe from interruptions and lunch regularly with interesting colleagues, while wearing something other than ratty gym clothes.

Nope. I'm still attempting to churn out journalistic masterpieces in the midst of domestic chaos. In the long run, I couldn't give up the "sick days" when my son and I watch videos or play games, the important conversations my daughter and I have over after-school snacks, the summer afternoons when I drop work and we all hike, visit a museum, or hit the pool. My work and family life are woven together, a kind of crazy quilt that keeps us all warm and happy, even if the pattern is a little offbeat and it sometimes threatens to come apart at the seams.

The ideal situation? I think all working moms would agree that it just doesn't exist. But on days when no one goes to the bathroom on the dog's head and the house doesn't burn down or flood, this one works for me.

Melanie Howard

In Mom We Trust

It was twenty years ago, but when I recall those days with my two daughters, I smile, and sometimes I sigh.

I had just moved to a new town. Michelle was thirteen and Heather was seven. That meant new schools for them, a new job for me. I took a sales and marketing job so that I could work out of my home and spend more time with them.

We were all going through a tough adjustment. The girls didn't understand that I was working now, even though I was at home. If I had to work in the evening, it was: "Oh, no, not another meeting." Phone messages got lost, and long faces were common.

Then I got an idea. I needed to somehow include them in my business. Get them on my team. So I came up with a plan. That night after dinner, I sat them down and explained my plan.

If I made my monthly business goals, then we would take 10 percent of my income and split it into three kitties. They each would get a third, and a third would go into a fund for taking a fun trip together. They didn't seem particularly impressed. Yawns and bored looks met my enthusiasm. That first month, I did manage to meet my goals, though the girls' attitudes remained about the same—until the day I sat them down again and counted out the money. We went to the bank and opened three savings accounts. I recommended that they save half and spend half of their third. We deposited the first payment into our trip account. Their eyes were wide. I had made an impact.

The second month, I noticed a difference. Phone messages would be printed out on my desk. Heather couldn't spell that well yet, but I will always remember one message: "Mary cant come to the meeding. Call her bak."

One day during that second month, I was having a hard time juggling all my roles and probably was experiencing some plain old depression because of my divorce. The girls came home from school and found me at my desk looking forlorn.

Michelle ran up to me. "Come on, Mom, get on the phone. It's only three o'clock! You've still got a few hours left." Her enthusiasm and energy were just what I needed, and I did just that.

Another night, I was worn out and told them I was going to bed right after dinner. I think they could tell I was having another low point. The next morning when I got up and walked into my office, I discovered that they had been busy while I slept. The flip chart that I sometimes used in sales presentations was open to a new page. On it they had copied a dollar bill, but then decided to make it a hundred dollar bill. Then instead of "In God We Trust," they had crossed out God and put "In Mom We Trust."

I was touched and tickled all at the same time. They were so pleased that they could cheer me on. We laughed and giggled about the poster. I left it up, and each time I saw it, I tried harder.

Months went by, and I began to succeed in my new field. I became the top salesperson in my group and then moved up to become a sales manager, which meant that I was responsible for other salespeople. I always told my story about my daughters and our teamwork. It helped and inspired others and always brought smiles.

In the beginning, the girls had been whining and complaining, now they were the steam in the engine of my train. I was a powerful force with those two behind me. Each month I met my goals, and we went through the ritual of dividing up the money, so they could save and spend theirs and we could save for our trip.

Michelle, a typical teenage girl, bought a lot of clothes, mostly pink. I kept my mouth shut because it was her money, and she was learning to manage it. Heather saved most of hers, though she did buy a guinea pig and later hamsters, including cages, exercise wheels, and other accessories. She was thrilled.

My daughters became respectful when I was working. I remember one day during a school break. I was on the phone and Heather and her best friend, Jennifer, were playing with a balloon in the living room, right next to my office. They were hitting the balloon back and forth and squealing in delight.

Then the phone rang in my office, and I picked it up. Without my saying a word, it was as if someone had pressed the mute button on the television. They were still batting the balloon, but without sound. I laughed out loud as I watched this scenario. As soon as I hung up the phone, the sound came back on.

We had begun our little experiment in January, and by summer, I was the top-producing person in my company. We were able to take a trip to visit my dad in Hawaii, paying for the tickets from our trip fund. As we sat on the plane, we all felt proud that we had worked for this and now could enjoy it together. I thanked them again for their support and encouragement.

As time went on, I noticed other advantages of their being a part of my business. When Heather sold Girl Scout cookies, she wanted to earn a T-shirt, which meant she had to sell seventy-five boxes. She had been sick and had only a few days left to accomplish her task.

She called Jennifer and Jennifer's brother Phillip to come over and help her. They took over my desk and sold the cookies just the way I had been doing my business for months—on the phone. They called all the relatives they could think of. Grandpa Don in Hawaii was first. "Hello, Grandpa Don, this is Heather. I'm selling Girls Scout cookies, and I was wondering how many boxes I can send to you. We can ship them."

I heard myself echoed in her words and actions. Not only that, but she became the sales manager, having her friends call their grandparents and sell to them. At the end of three hours and much hilarity, they had sold all seventy-five boxes!

When a little girl knocked on our door asking if we wanted to buy cookies, Heather looked at me and said, "Mom, she's doing it the hard way."

My working at home had started out as a difficult situation, but it became a delightful way for us to share my work and for the girls to learn about business. Heather ended up saving enough money so that years later, when she graduated from college, she was able to go to Europe.

Even now, twenty years later, I still smile when I remember those sweet days. We were all learning so much—so much was new. And having one another and being a team made it a rich, full, and fun experience. I cherish those memories. And both my daughters became successful businesswomen.

I like to think it all started with "In Mom We Trust."

Diane M. Covington

"Here's your schedule that you set for today, ma'am.
At 10 AM, board meeting . . . noon, client lunch . . . 2:00,
staff meeting . . . 3:00, call home and yell at the kids for
not doing homework . . . 3:05, feel guilty . . . 5:00, go
home and apologize to kids . . ."

Notes Left by Two Working Parents

Monday
Sweetheart,

It's Claire's turn to bring snacks to school today. There's celery in the fridge. Cut it up into two-inch chunks, spread peanut butter on them, and place five raisins on each. Wrap in cellophane (not a dry cleaners bag!), and be sure there are twenty-four, plus one for her teacher, Ms. Goodesteem. Tidy the family room if you get a chance. Did you call the plumber yet?

I love you,
Allison

Monday
Honey,

That was okra not celery. Claire saw me spreading Cheez Whiz on them and cried twenty minutes until I forked over twenty-four pieces of Halloween candy (who told the kids the candy was hidden in the vacuum bag?). By the time I untied your son's double knots with your graduation pen, the family room was a lost cause. Dinner is on time bake. I have Rotary tonight. Was the pen important?

Hugs and kisses,
Ken

Tuesday

Ken,

The toilet has been asking for the plumber. You forgot Alasdair's milk money again. He says he owes some fifth grader $3.25 plus interest for milk loans. I have a meeting tonight. The mess has spread to the dining room.

Love,
Allison

Tuesday

Allison,

I couldn't find Alasdair's lunch box, so I used your hat. Call the principal about the loan shark. Replaced your graduation pen—disregard the year. I think you took my car keys this morning—the taxi's here, got to go.

Sincerely,
Ken

Wednesday

Hey,

Your keys were in the juice pitcher. The kids won't go to the bathroom—when's the plumber coming? I enjoyed our talk last night. We have to abandon the downstairs to the clutter and take refuge upstairs tonight. Dinner is on your son's top bunk.

Allison

Wednesday

Al,

We didn't have a conversation last night—our bed was full of kids; I slept with the dog. What's the plumber's phone number? Did you know Tuesday was class picture day, and your son wore his "I'm with Stupid" T-shirt . . . apparently he stood next to his teacher.

Ken

Thursday

The neighbor called—something about your son and some jumper cables. I said you'd stop by tonight and talk to them. I spoke with the principal, picture retakes are next Monday. . . . I burned the shirt. We owe the principal $4.50 for loaning our son milk money, too.

A.

Thursday

Yesterday was Alasdair's snack day. Luckily, I had gum. I promise I'll call the plumber today.

K.

Friday

Wife,

I had a breakfast meeting this morning. I sandbagged the bathroom last night; call the National Guard if it crests. Any idea where the cat is?

Me

Friday

Husband,

Provisions are low, and something is moving in the living room—could be the cat. Order pizza and watch out for the waterfall on the stairs.

P.S. Bring your sleeping bag; we're in the attic divvying up the rest of the Halloween candy.

Ken Swarner

There's No Such Thing
as a Part-Time Mom

When my oldest children, Jennifer and Tiffany, were small, I agreed to work three mornings a week at their preschool. This meant the exhausting routine of having two small bodies in the car and ready to go by seven forty-five on these mornings. Still, the preschool let out at eleven thirty, so I happily thought there would be plenty of day left to get everything else done.

It wasn't long until I realized a fly was in this sweet ointment. What worked so well in my head, soon paled in the face of reality. Working part-time took more time than I'd planned. There were meetings at school and preparations to be made for the next day. We rarely left the school before noon.

I thought it made sense to go grocery shopping on the way home from school. The children had eaten a mid-morning snack, and I assumed it would hold them through an hour of shopping. What I didn't ask was what would hold me through an hour of shopping?

I'd spent three hours with lively four-year-olds. I was tired and hungry. Now I'd dragged along two tired children who took up half the grocery cart and wanted everything from toaster treats to corn dogs. Those sounded pretty good to me, too. Unfortunately, my budget bit the dust as did my waistline.

My oldest girl loved to "mommy" her sister. On one fateful trip, I unloaded the girls at the checkout and fixed my attention on the groceries. In less than a minute, the two-year-old began to wail, and I turned to see her clasped in a bear hug.

"Let go of your sister," I told my four-year-old.

She sighed, looking as though I was making a big mistake. "She wouldn't leave the candy alone."

She let go, and Tiffany gnawed through a chocolate bar, which was added to the tab.

On the next trip, I bought them gumballs from the machine. My oldest daughter loved to put in the money and take out the balls. This time her small hand proved unequal to the task. Of the two large balls, one rolled across the floor.

"Oops," she said, "Tiffany's is gone."

Tiffany wailed. We got more gumballs. An unequal number was the result. I had to chew the third to avoid more tears. My jaws were locked for a week.

By now, I was smart enough to know I had to adjust my thinking. I didn't tackle the store on the way home from school anymore. We shopped on one of the mornings we had story hour and playgroups. Life was busy.

That left my other day off for cleaning. The girls knew it was coming. We did it every week. Yet every time, it came as a surprise. I told them to pick up their toys and be ready by the time I got to their room. As I vacuumed the hall, coming ever nearer their doorway, the screams would begin.

"Hurry! Hurry! She's coming," Jennifer would yell.

Tiffany would cry and crawl atop the bed.

I felt like Attila the Hun.

I'd turn off the vacuum to find they'd been playing the whole time. The room was a mess, toys scattered all over the floor and Jennifer trying frantically to rescue them at the last minute from the noisy jaws of death.

I'd sigh and give them a little longer to clean up.

Three mornings a week had sounded so reasonable when I signed on. What I hadn't counted on was that whatever time I spent at work had to be made up at home. I spent the girls' nap time on lesson planning, so we did things together when they awoke.

Gradually, I learned to work the job around my family.

And that's what I've continued to do. I've discovered, whether through part-time or full-time work, families are a full-time job.

The kids are older and the activities are different. And somehow we have adjusted, some days more smoothly than others. I work full time now. Yet I know when I get home, there will be full-time parenting and full-time housework.

Forgotten notes for cookies come at the last minute, and driving lessons conflict with work schedules. Yet it all works out.

Moms have the incredible ability to morph to meet the needs of their families. Perhaps it's magic. Or perhaps it's determination.

Whatever it is, it lies in the soul of a working mom.

Karen Cogan

The Best of Both Worlds

I realized returning to the working world with four children, Bob, Demi, Kaila, and Drew, would be challenging. I had completed my teaching degree and felt prepared to start a new phase of my life. The house was organized, child care arranged, and meals premade in the freezer. I worked the week prior to the first day of school, and my children came with me to help me decorate my new classroom. What could possibly be difficult about being a working mom? If everything went according to plan, I could manage to have the best of both worlds. Life was good.

The first day of school arrived all too quickly. Everyone laid in restless anticipation the night before. Bob, in high school, wondered how tough his classes would be and if homework would once again cramp his social life. My fashion queens, Demi and Kaila, had fussed for many hours during the day over the dilemma of what to wear on the first day of school; now they laid awake wondering if they made the right choices. I lay worrying over all the minute details of teaching rambunctious middle school students, and more important, if my own children would be able to adjust to my working. After all, my children had been used to a stay-at-home mom for several years now;

how would they manage? Drew, my preschooler, was the only heavy sleeper of the family. He snoozed, exhausted from a day of play—the bliss of being young and worry-free.

The alarm buzzed and the adventure began. Bob actually got out of bed on my second wake-up reminder. If my high schooler could move out of the comfort of his bed with plenty of time to catch the bus, it was a sign the day was going to go well. Backpacks and lunches for Demi and Kaila had been packed the night before. After only a few anxious moments about their fashion statements, they were ready for the before-school program. Drew enjoyed playing with friends at preschool, so he was always ready and set for another day of LEGOs, crayons, and playground fun.

My school day started earlier than the children's, and with factoring in time for dropping Drew off at preschool, there would be about two hours the girls would be alone in the morning and then about a half hour in the afternoon. I had enrolled them in the before-school program, but had decided to let them gain some responsibility by staying home alone in the afternoon; Bob had an after-school job.

I experienced several moments of doubt as I said good-bye to each of my children, but it was too late to change the new voyage we were beginning. Demi and Kaila settled in with the other children, chatting and participating in activities. Demi is a "type-A worrier," though, and was concerned about being late, so she watched the clock move toward the time the bell would ring signifying it was time to line up for the day. She went to use the restroom just prior to the bell. As she was finishing, the bell rang, so out of fear of being late, she moved rapidly from the stall, painfully slamming her finger against the door in the process. All day she suffered intense pain as her broken finger swelled. She was afraid to mention it to anyone because she knew I was not home and didn't know what would happen to her.

Thankfully, my first day ended as quickly as it had

begun. Teaching is a lot like motherhood—both are synonyms for multitasking. Drew greeted me with a big hug when I arrived at his school. I quickly drove home to check on Demi and Kaila. Kaila had a big smile and lots to share about her day; however, when I looked at Demi, she burst into tears. Through sobs she told me about her finger and showed me a swollen mass. A rapid drive to the doctor and radiologist resulted in confirmation that her finger was broken.

Okay, so the first day had a few "bumps," but surely the second day would go smoother. The day started off similar to the first with the exception that Bob needed multiple reminders to get out of bed, and even then he barely made it to school on time. I reassured Demi that she was more important than my job and to share with her teacher if something comes up again. There were lots of good-bye hugs for all; then off we went.

I returned home with Drew after a full day of teaching challenges to find Demi and Kaila in the kitchen looking rather sheepish. Now what? They both started to talk at once. Kaila had wanted an after-school snack and had decided to heat some beans. She knew she was not allowed to use the stove, so she opened the can, put the beans in a metal pot and then into the microwave. Sparks started flying immediately. Demi stopped it, but even those few seconds was enough to damage the microwave. At that point there was nothing to do but laugh at how challenging our lives had become.

Any thought I previously had about it being easy to be a working mom was erased and replaced with the uncertainty of never knowing what was going to happen next. There are times when all a working mom can do is laugh, hug the kids, and then move on to the next moment of chaos, which is sure to occur.

Debi Callies

The Glamorous Life as a Novelist

It was the Post-it-covered dog that finally did me in.

What made me think I could work from a home office? Work an eight-hour day as a novelist and simultaneously rear four children, not to mention the incorrigible corgi, the pet python, the noisy cockatoo, and the small flock of lovebirds. I thought I could juggle it all. I thought I could have balance, but I now realize balance is as big a piece of fiction as my books.

The most ironic thing of all, of course, is I write chick lit. You know, those books about cosmo-sipping socialites or single women in the city. They have a lot of sex, and none of it is interrupted by a six-year-old poised midvomit saying, "I don't feeeeeeeeel good, Mommy." My heroines wear designer shoes and never have to think about how utterly impractical four-hundred-dollar high heels are. My books' titles are snappy, *Mafia Chic* and *Spanish Disco*. My covers are glossy, with gorgeous women, not one of whom has a baby spit-up stain on her silk blouse.

But my real life, my very real life, is rather like walking a tightrope without a net.

So it was today. While I have the luxury of getting to work from home, my day reads rather like most working moms' days: Wake up at a brutally early hour, start the coffeemaker, wake up child number one, the high schooler who despises early mornings and greets me with rudeness. Pour large cup of coffee with creamer and sugar added; start chugging said coffee. Go back to the door of high schooler's bedroom and scream, "Get up before you miss the bus!" Go plead with husband, "She won't get up. You try." Drink more coffee. Wake up children numbers two and three. Child number two turns on cartoons. Yell at child number two to turn them off because he is incapable of putting on socks while SpongeBob is on. Gets too distracted. Drink more coffee. Child number one leaves house—slamming door. Say a prayer, "Please let her make the bus." Look at watch. Shake head. How can it be I've been up for less than twenty minutes?

Baby awakes by screaming from his crib to let us all know the Little Prince of the house (midlife baby means he's much younger, and everyone dotes on him) wants up now! Change diaper. Hoist him into kitchen, set him in high chair, toss Cheerios on tray before he screams more. Check on child number two—mesmerized by SpongeBob. Child number three needs to be pulled into upright position to wake her. Give up and start dressing her while she's still asleep.

Fast forward through more coffee and now leaving to drive children two and three to school. Get baby in car seat, children in seat belts. Back out of driveway. Drive three feet. Child number two says, "It's band today! I have to get my baritone." (Note: baritone is not the most melodious of instruments for beginners.) Stop car. Child runs for instrument. By the time he gets back into car and into seat belt, we now will be right in the midst of rush hour traffic—I've lost my five-minute buffer.

Somehow, kids get to school. Drive home, make another pot of coffee. Baby is settled with rattles and toys. Phone rings. It's the school. Child two forgot lunch; child three has a stomachache and a temperature. Grab the lunch, the baby; drive to school. Exchange one lunch for one child. Go home.

For expediency of this story, fast forward through five hours of trying to write about glamorous lives of my heroines with their hunky boyfriends who do not, I repeat, *do not*, leave their underwear on the floor, who will ask for directions, and who know how to change a roll of toilet paper. Husband needs lessons.

Manage to write a whopping five pages. Agent calls. "How's the book going?"

"Oh, you know, it's going."

"You're going to meet your deadline, right?"

"Of course." Add airy little, "Ha, ha, ha. Of course!"

Hang up. Panic. Type faster.

Child number one comes home, complains there's "nothing good" in the fridge. Child number two needs to be picked up. Retrieve him. While gone, baby coats dog in Post-its while high schooler was supposed to be watching him. She has burned a bag of microwave popcorn, giving house strange and disgusting burnt odor.

Try to write. Feel stuck. Blocked. No words come. Go into bathroom and lock door so I can think.

Deep breaths. You can make this deadline.

Note passed under door from child number two, with pencil attached.

> *Dear Mom:*
> *I love you. Can I invite Tim over for a playdate?*
> *Check one:*
> *YES   NO*
> *Thanks,*
> *Your son, Nick*

Check off yes, because really my day is shot anyway. Slide paper back under door.

Bang, bang on the door.

"Yes?"

"I have to 'frow up." Child number three.

Vacate bathroom as safe location to escape.

Clean up after sick child number three. Tuck her in bed with ginger ale.

Fast forward through a dinner from someplace with a drive-thru window, homework, baritone practice, three diaper changes, four loads of laundry, and a fast vacuum of Cheerios scattered throughout living room.

Husband says, "Do you know you have food in your hair?"

I say, "Do you know you left your underwear on the floor this morning?"

"I like you with food in your hair. Reminds me why I love you. You're beautiful, you know."

Try to decide whether to kiss him or kill him.

Check on children. Tuck baby in. He says first word. "Mama."

Melt.

Decide it's all worth it.

Then decide there is no balance. There is no having it all. Scratch that. There is if you believe life isn't like the glossy book covers. If you decide to trade cosmos for Cheerios. If you realize life is messy around the edges. If you think sticky kisses and hugs are more important than pristine, power silk blouses. If you are willing to trade a little of your 401(k) for homemade cards and bouquets of dandelions. If you don't mind Post-its on the dog and handprints on the walls. This is my life.

My glamorous life.

And I wouldn't trade it for all the Manolos and bright pink cosmos in the world!

Erica Orloff

Of Mice, Men, and the *New York Times*

"You're so lucky to work at home!" That was the refrain
I heard so often in my life as a freelance writer–mom, especially when our daughters were young.

Yes, I was lucky. Sometimes.

But with that luck came a few challenges.

Case in point: Some years ago, when I was just starting
to feel my oats as a fledgling journalist who had conquered
community newspapers, then had gone on to magazines
and regional publications, along came the big breakthrough—an assignment for the mighty *New York Times'*
Sunday New Jersey section.

Okay, I was nervous. This was, after all, the country's
newspaper of record. And I wanted to shine—absolutely
dazzle my editor and all those readers.

The subject required heavy interviews. Lots of them.
But the lynchpin—the central source—was a highly
accomplished scientist with an international reputation, a
man of spectacular credentials and a seventeen-page
resume.

So, of course, I carefully scheduled the interview at a
time when my three children, then all under the age of
nine, would be out of the house. I felt triumphant. Things

were falling right into place. That is, until I got a phone call from the scientist's assistant on the morning of the interview announcing that we had to change the time to later in the day.

Seems that the scientist—a doctor and my interviewee—was behind schedule. He was also flying out of the country that very evening, so there was no other chance for our interview, except for that tumultuous hour just after the kids got home from school.

I called every friend I knew. And nobody could help out with my three little darlings that afternoon.

I ran through the list of babysitters with the same result.

I even called my mother and sister, who live an hour away, but they, too, were totally unavailable.

I can still remember the race to pick up our three daughters from their two schools that afternoon, and the lecture that began in the car: Mommy has a very, very important phone call to make. She needs your cooperation. She is counting on it.

No interruptions. No fighting. Just three little angels permitted, on this day of days, to watch lots of television in the family room, coupled with promises of special desserts for one and all.

My daughters listened earnestly, pledged their absolute cooperation in this high-level matter, and even conned me into a promise of staying up a bit later in view of the high stakes.

At precisely 4:00 PM the phone rang, and I was told that the doctor was ready for the interview. I was seated at my desk in the room we euphemistically called my home office, and my computer was at the ready.

I could exhale.

Until, out of that special place in a mother's brain, I heard sounds I didn't like. Sounds of stifled screams. Sounds of crisis.

I think I actually started praying as I pushed on. *Just let me finish this interview, Lord, and I'll never ask for anything else. . . ."*

Seconds later, as the brainy scientist was getting to the precise core issue, the door opened and three little girls came bursting in. It would have been impossible for my subject not to hear their cries.

Seems that they had been in the kitchen for some extra snacks when they saw something small and gray dart from behind the refrigerator. That something was a mouse. And that mouse now had the run of the house.

There are no guidelines taught in journalism school for how to handle this sort of thing. There are no primers in Mouse Interruption 101.

Let me cut to the chase: I asked the famous scientist who had a plane to catch to please wait while I—ahem—settled a small problem.

I ran with my three daughters to the master bathroom, clutching my cordless phone as if it were the hidden treasure of the Sierra Madre.

With Jill, Amy, and Nancy shrieking, I slammed shut the door, and all four of us crowded into the bathtub. Yes, the bathtub. It felt safe.

It was from there that I resumed my interview, taking notes on the back of a magazine, and in the margins of its pages, all the while imagining what the *New York Times* assigning editor would make of my—ahem—professionalism.

The scientist couldn't have been nicer. And, yes, I did explain the crisis to a man who turned out to have a delightful sense of humor—and the suggestion that mice love peanut butter, so we might try that in a trap.

I wrote the story and sent it in. It made it into print. And the mouse was never seen again, peanut butter traps aside.

I have never forgotten my mommy-in-the-bathtub

caper. And I have been forever humbled by the grace of the mighty—in this case, a scientist who could not have been more understanding of a frantic journalist who was also a mommy.

And no matter how many interviews have followed that one, it will always be a reminder of this eternal verity: when it comes to mommies—and work—count on nothing predictable, and just go with the flow—even if it takes you into the bathtub.

Sally Friedman

"There's someone to see you about a buy out."

Morning Glory

When I was young, my father woke us up some mornings. He would come into our rooms singing, "Good morning to you, good morning to you, we're all in our places, with bright shining faces, oh, what a good way to start a new day!" Other days my mother would wake us up singing, "Hey, what do you know, it's morning already, here comes the sun. . . ." What nice parents I had! Well, until I turned fifteen, anyway. I don't know what happened to them then. They got better again later, about the time I turned twenty, I think. Guess they just had a bad spell for a few years.

Having been awakened in such a pleasant way every day of my formative years, you can be pretty certain that I make sure my children start their days off in a similar way. I would like for you to think so; in fact, I encourage it. Imagine me, up, scrubbed, dressed in an *I Love Lucy*-type morning outfit, carrying a tray to each of my children, with something hot and sweet to drink and a bud vase with a daffodil in it bobbing its head festively. Go on thinking that. Just don't bet any large amounts of money on it. Mornings around here are not unpleasant, depending on your tolerance for noise and hullabaloo, but they don't start off with singing.

Here's how it is on a day I don't work—because when I do work, I leave early and I have no idea how they get bathed and dressed and fed without me. Both my husband and I are early risers. Typically, I will have been up long enough in the morning to have become pretty deeply involved in some project before it is time to wake up the kids. Then I will suddenly realize that it is ten minutes until seven and we are late.

I screech. Why? Because I usually don't want to quit what I am doing. So instead of "Good morning to you," I shriek, "Wake up! Feet on the floor! You're late!" I think this is a very effective way to wake up the children. Not only does it rouse them, but also it scares the pudding out of them and their little hearts pitty-pat from 60 beats a minute straight to a respectable 160 beats a minute. This is bound to be good for their cardiovascular health. Plus they get a massive dose of good old vitamin A—as in adrenaline—right off the bat. This has the happy side effect of completely clearing their heads of any residual sleepiness. They are up, they are pumped, and they are ready for battle.

Forget orange juice, the double shot of fight or flight juice my kids get is a great way for them to start the day. Not only are they wide-awake and raring to go, but also they are in the right mind-set for the great bathroom battle. We have an old house with nice big bedrooms and lots of sunshine and windows and a great big yard. And one shower. We have tried to compensate for this with an enormous water heater, but still you don't want to be the last guy in line. Things are a little better now that the girls are gone most of the time. They took the art of makeup application to new heights, often taking upwards of thirty minutes to perfect the all-natural look they preferred. With them gone, much more time is available for the boys to do whatever it is they do in there that takes so long. I know for a fact that they are not spending all that time on their teeth.

Every day as they start to leave the house, I kiss them and then I ask, "Did you brush your teeth?" Every single day they get the same shocked look on their faces. "Teeth? Do I have teeth? Am I supposed to—what was that word you used?—brrrrruuuussshhh them? Oh my! Who'd've thunk?" And then off they pound, up the stairs (which surely cannot survive too many more years of such violent use), where they shove and elbow and insult each other, splash water and gargle noisily and, I am pretty sure, wet those brushes, give each other a conspiratorial wink, and pound back down and out the door.

Have a nice day!

Elizabeth Bussey Sowdal

6

THROUGH THE
EYES OF A CHILD

*There are only two things a child will share
willingly; communicable diseases and its
mother's age.*

A Child's Playground

A child's playground could be anywhere—a backyard, the sidewalk, a ball field, a nursing home. A nursing home?

That's exactly where I spent my afternoons as an eight-year-old. The red brick building, whose back door opened up into our church parking lot, had been the local medical clinic until a modern hospital opened just a mile down the road.

When the new hospital opened, my mother informed me of another business opening in its former residence. It would be called a convalescent center. Those were mighty big words for an eight-year-old.

"A what?"

"A convalescent center. It's like a hospital but only for older people."

I had no reason to question my mother on this subject, especially after learning that she would be working at the conva... well, nursing home, which was what everyone else called it. This would be her first job, at least since I could remember, and would most likely alter my everyday routine. Coupled with the departure of my sister, who married earlier that year, this was really going to shake up my world.

Luckily, the nursing home was a short distance from school, which allowed me to walk there some afternoons. At first I enjoyed my visits—learning about my mother's job and getting to know the patients. My mother walked me down the hall and into the individual rooms, introducing me to the occupants of each bed. Some I knew already, many by name, most by association with their families.

Few patients were mobile; most were not able to venture out of their beds or much farther than a nearby chair. Many could not feed themselves or tend to their personal needs without at least some assistance. Others could not even express themselves well enough to make their wants and wishes known.

Always spreading cheer, Mother was an angel-in-waiting to many of the patients, and I was the tagalong on her shirttail. I would peep around from behind her, too shy to speak aloud, when she introduced me even to those who couldn't see beyond the foot of their beds. Some couldn't remember my name after I left.

Still, I enjoyed seeing the wrinkled faces light up as Mom entered each room. When I tired of being a shadow, I would sit in the front waiting room, which retained its clinical aroma. It was there that I met my friend.

She was old, though at age eight I couldn't tell the difference between a fifty-year-old and a ninety-year-old. To a child there is no degree of old, just old. The skin of her face was wrinkled, and her hair was white, two of my prerequisites for old age. What made her different was the way she moved about, as though she were dutifully carrying out a task and stopping only long enough to check on the child sitting alone in the brown Naugahyde chair. I rubbed my hands along the silver metal arms that appeared more like the guardrails on the patients' beds.

Pausing in front of the chair and peering from up above

me like the Grinch looking down over Whoville, she grabbed under my arms and hoisted me into the air before settling into the chair herself and plopping me onto her lap. Story after story she told until I became antsy and bolted, sprinting down the hall to find my mother.

Occasionally, my friend chased after me, and I would discard my shoes, sliding down the hall in stocking feet until a heavy wooden door or a concrete wall blocked my path. When the hallway wasn't my track, it was my playing field. I sometimes brought my own playthings, like a rubber baseball or a miniature football that she tossed to me as I slid down the hall and made diving catches up against the wall.

Having to retrieve an errant pass or fumble, I frequently ventured into various rooms where I happened upon surprised but delighted patients who were pleased to be visited by an eight-year-old with a football in tow. Lonely and longing to belong, many were happy to be visited by anyone.

In that year, I'd learned more about life than school had taught me about any subject. From the men and women in those rooms, I learned that what we need most is one another. From my mother, I saw that one caring soul can make a difference in the health and happiness of others. From my friend, I learned that age doesn't matter, and the differences in people when measured by age is far less than we envision.

One year later I grew from an atypical eight-year-old into a typical nine-year-old. At that age, one year represents a generation of transformations. The time came for my mind to wander and my interests to change. After-school playtime with friends and neighbors took priority and captured the place of my trips to the nursing home. My visits became sporadic and eventually ended.

Never forgetting that year of fun and frolic in the nursing

home, my mother kept me abreast of the latest proceedings on a regular basis. Occasionally, I would inquire about the status of certain individuals, particularly those who were related to my friends and classmates. Some were doing well, some weren't, and some had passed to a better place.

Remembering my friend and worried that she may have died, I asked my mother if the patient I used to play with was still alive. If so, I wanted to know how she was doing.

She gazed at me with a quizzical look on her face. "Which patient?"

"You know. The white-haired lady that used to play ball with me and tell me stories."

Quickly her appearance transformed to one of comical disbelief. "Son, she wasn't a patient. That lady was the director. She was my boss."

I was humiliated. Maybe I should have guessed because of her behavior, but I based my assumption on how she looked, which to me was "old."

Through the years, my nursing home days found protective shelter far back into my recollection. High school passed and college arrived, while that year in the nursing home was hidden from my thoughts, only to be revived on the evening news.

The year was 1976 and I was home for a few weeks, taking a break from college studies. One Saturday evening our family was relaxing in the den with the television on, although no one was watching closely.

Reading the paper, I glanced up if something caught my attention. While sewing, mother occasionally peeked up at the screen, only to go right back to her task.

Suddenly, she pointed at the screen and looked over at me. "Do you recognize her?"

Not really paying attention, I asked, "Who?"

"Her." She pointed at the white-haired lady being interviewed by the newsman. "Do you remember her?"

"Not really," was my honest answer. I had seen her on television before, but as far as knowing her personally, I couldn't say that I did.

"That's the lady you used to play with at the nursing home. Remember now?"

I did. Her face and mannerisms were no different than they were thirteen years earlier. She still seemed vibrant and active, nevertheless she looked old. A chill came over me as I realized this was the same woman that used to tell me stories as I sat in her lap and chased me down the hall, laughing as I slid and crashed into the wall.

Now, here she was on the national news. They called her Miss Lillian. She was helping her son Jimmy Carter campaign for president of the United States.

Tony Gilbert

We're Out of Food

"Someone had better be bleeding, or there must be fire somewhere in the house before you call me again." How many of us working moms have told that to our kids after the umpteenth time of being interrupted at work?

When I first began to let my boys, Jason and Justin, stay alone after school, I told them to call my office and tell me when they arrived home from school. After that, they were only to call in an emergency. I explained to them that I was busy at work and could not be taking phone calls every few minutes. Yet over and over the phone would ring with both of them on an extension trying to explain to me at the same time what the other had done wrong. We would go over the rules again, and the calls might stop for a while.

The real topper came the day I was called out of a meeting with the message that my son was on the telephone with an emergency. Of course, my stomach sank, and I hurried for my phone. I answered, only to have Jason inform me that we had no food in the house and they had nothing to eat. As my stomach settled back into place and my heart quit pounding, I explained that there was plenty of food in the house. "But we have no chips," he responded.

Apparently in the eyes of a boy, when you have no potato chips, you have no food. At the time I was not very pleased with him, and I'm sure that by the time I hung up and returned to my meeting, he was aware of my displeasure.

Over the years, as my sons have grown up and moved out on their own, the thought of that phone call brings laughter to my heart. I guess it is important for us moms to remember that adults and children may have very different views of what constitutes an emergency.

My boys share an apartment these days. Maybe I'll swing by and drop off a couple of bags of chips, just in case they are out of food!

Pamela Teague

The Value of Money

Reality leaves a lot to the imagination.

John Lennon

It was almost over. Today was the last day of my maternity leave, and tomorrow I would have to be courageous enough to head back to work.

I had been off work for twelve weeks after the birth of our second, and probably last, child. You might think that maternity leave would be about the baby, the new baby, and for the first few weeks that was probably the case. But my maternity leave turned into a magical vacation with my "almost" three-year-old.

Every week we tried to go on a special outing, trips that would create memories for both of us that would fuel smiles for years to come. But the mundane daily activities, such as trips to the store and after-dinner walks, were what made the days so special. Who would have realized the joy in the exuberant flinging of handfuls of maple seeds—helicopters—high into the air again and again? Or the beauty of the moment when that small hand reached unconsciously up for yours, then gripped it tightly, even when you weren't crossing the street? And also the pride you felt as you got to see the quiet growth of your child's mind. That summer also saw the blossoming curiosity and the ceaseless "why?" "how?" and "then what?" questions that lead a mind from baby thoughts to adult thinking.

The last week that I was off, I had been trying to help prepare her, and myself, for the end of this idyll. I would casually mention that next week I would be going to work in the morning and she would get to spend the day with Daddy until preschool started. Sometimes this brought no response, but frequently she would ask why I had to return to work. My response, "To earn money," evoked the "Why do we need money?" question, which led to the "To pay for the house and the car and food" answer.

Today was Sunday, and the three of us were headed to the grocery store to stock up for the whole week because we wouldn't be able to make quick runs after lunch during the week anymore. Part of our store ritual was to take a little change from the car in with us to buy a lemonade to share on our trip through the store.

As she was climbing into the van to go, she found a quarter on the floor and exclaimed in delight, "Oh, I found a piece of money!"

I asked, "What will you buy with it?" expecting an answer of a seahorse from the aquarium or lemonade, her frequent answers to this question.

But today she looked at me solemnly and replied, "A house and car."

I was stunned for a second, then I gave my usual response, "Why that?"

She stated, "So you don't have to go back to work, Mommy."

She was quiet on the way to the store, two miles from our house. So was I.

When we got there, I collected a second quarter from

the van and handed it to her for our lemonade, then lifted her out and into a cart and headed into the store.

We stopped in front of the machine, and I waited for her to feed the quarters in to get a lemonade. She used the quarter I had given her, but kept the one she had found clenched in her fist.

Since I had taken only one quarter from the van, I explained to her that we didn't have enough money to buy a lemonade without the other quarter. She wouldn't give it up because she still needed to "Buy a house and car with it." I tried a few more times, but she would not give up that quarter. And rather than whining for the treat, a more typical toddler reaction, she was perfectly cheerful not having her special treat that day because the quarter she had found had a higher purpose.

Needless to say, when I got an opportunity, I acquired that 1985 quarter from her and brought it with me on my first day back to work as a souvenir of that golden moment of innocent faith and confidence.

Lynda Johnson

"I bet business would improve, Katie,
if you had a "Junior Citizen's discount.""

Out of the Mouths of Babes

As a busy working mother of an infant and kindergartner, my daughter, Betsy, juggles her aerospace engineer career and motherhood. Her following e-mail to me contains some thoughts for working moms:

I talked to a guy at work who's been married for thirty-four years. His two sons are grown and gone. He talked about how fast time goes by and how parents have to make sacrifices. You can't turn the clock back. I'm working full time, maybe more. I may take the risk and go part-time in the fall. Amy will be out of school at three o'clock, so maybe I could work five hours a day and be there to pick her up. I asked her this morning what she'd like, and she said she'd like me to be there. I told her my options—how I could work less—we would get less money—but we would have more time together. She said, "But I'm special-er than money!" Out of the mouths of babes.

Miriam Hill

Too Much Work

Going back to work after a few years of being a stay-at-home mom was more of a challenge than I had anticipated. My days seemed to consist of running to work, running to school, running to the grocery store, and running up and down the stairs doing laundry and cleaning. My list of things to do seemed endless.

In the middle of one such day, frazzled and worn out, I decided that my daughters, who were then ages six, five, and three, could start helping. I had them pick up their toys in their bedrooms, make their beds, and do a couple of other small tasks. I left them in their bedrooms to finish their assignments. When I came back to check on them, I was amused and a little exasperated to overhear them grumbling to one another, "How come we have to do all the work?"

Cynthia Morningstar

What's in It for Us Is Good

I am a classroom teacher, and the majority of my students' mothers work outside the home, which is quite different from when I started teaching twenty years ago. Then, most of my students' mothers were stay-at-home moms.

After school, the children are enrolled in child-care programs, go to a friend's house, or stay home with an older brother or sister, a grandparent, or a hired babysitter. I often wondered how the children felt about this, so one day I asked a combined fourth- and fifth-grade group. Here is a representative sampling of their responses:

Kevin: My mom is a lab technician. I feel it's a good opportunity for her. Even though I don't see her as much as I'd like to, I know it's the right decision for her, and if she likes it, she should keep doing it. If she doesn't like it, she should go out and find another job she's capable of.

Antonio: My mom runs a beauty shop, and I think it's fine for mothers to work. It should be their decision. It's their life.

Jenna: Women have just as much right to work as men because there really isn't that much difference between a boy and girl except for their body parts. It's what's inside their bodies that counts.

Ezra: Well, I think moms should stay home with their kids; otherwise, the kids might think the mom loves her job more than she loves her kids.

Dori: Kids might think they're loved a little more if their moms don't work, but if they do work, I know I understand, and a lot of kids understand. My parents love me as much as they would if they weren't both working.

Ricky: My mom doesn't work, but I wish she did. Then I could see my dad more. I see my mom too much, and I'm getting a little tired of seeing her so much. I don't see enough of my dad.

Andrew: I think it's good if mothers work. My mom works and there's no problem with it. Anyone can work, even kids. If you're a kid, you can have a paper route or shovel snow. And if you're a mom, you can work, too. It's not just dads who can work. And when I have to stay home, it's okay. I take care of my sister, and I don't feel uncomfortable at all. I feel it's good for moms to work so they can get more money for the family.

Ned: I don't mind my mom working at all 'cause I can do whatever I want to when she's not home.

Annie: Well, I do mind 'cause every day after school, my brother beats me up!

Cindy: I don't really care that my mom works, but I like it when she's home, because I like to be home with my mom.

Lenny: My mom is a policewoman. She has always worked, so I don't know what it would be like if she didn't.

Terry: Mine didn't start working until I was in second grade. At first, it felt kind of strange coming home and not having her there waiting for me. So that's another point. It's kind of a change for kids when the mom didn't work and then she goes into working. You're not used to her not being there when you come home. You're used to seeing her standing at the door saying, "How was your day?"

Paul: Well, I think mothers should work, because if they don't, we're going right back into, like, two hundred years ago, when only the men worked. In some places, even now, only the men work, but I think women have every right to work if they want to.

Annie: I don't mind my mom working, but I just hardly ever see her. She works from 10:00 AM until 10:00 PM at my dad's restaurant and on weekends, too. I stay with my grandma. I just wish my mom could arrange something so she didn't have to work so much. It's okay for moms to work, but they should have some time to spend with their children—and the dads should, too.

Susie: It also depends on what the parents' choice is, because sometimes they don't go to bed until twelve or one, and then they both have to get up real early to go to work, and then they're too tired and cranky to spend time with their kids when they do get home from work. And on weekends, they just lie around and take naps—dads, too.

Jeremy: My parents might not be able to spend as much time with my brother and me as we'd like them to 'cause they both have to work. But if they didn't work, we wouldn't have a house—we'd be on the streets. If they didn't work, we wouldn't have good food or be able to take family vacations. So what's in it for us is good.

I realized from our discussion that the most important thing in children's minds today, or at least at my school, doesn't seem to be how much time mothers spend at home with their children, but rather, how mothers feel about working, and also, the financial benefits to the whole family from mothers working. What really seems to matter to children today is that Mom and Dad are there for them emotionally and that they show that they love and care about them.

Arlene Uslander

Hi Ho, Hi Ho, It's Off to Work I Go—Not

Well, it seemed like a typical morning in the Davis household. The alarm sounded at its usual 5:00 AM, and of course, I responded as I usually do—by hitting the snooze button. Normally, whenever the snooze button is hit, the alarm would sound every five minutes, so I would lie in bed and calculate in my head the number of times it snoozed, and then I would get up around 5:30 AM.

This particular day, something was wrong with either the clock or my counting, because when I heard it go off again, it was 6:45 and not 5:30. I jumped out of bed, pulling rollers out of my head and at the same time trying to undress for the shower. After showering and brushing my teeth, I hurried to dress and comb my hair. I prayed that my four- and two-year-old would cooperate and get washed and dressed without incident. Luckily, I had prepared their clothes and the lunches the night before as most working mothers do. Surprisingly, my two-year-old son awakened by himself and didn't put up much fuss when I washed him. Like most independent two-year-olds, he insisted on dressing himself without any help from me. As he dressed himself, I attempted to waken my four-year-old daughter. She wasn't too happy about getting up.

She went through her daily ritual of saying the days of the week so she could see how close the weekend was. She kept singing, "Sunday, Monday, Tuesday, Wednesday, Thursday, Friday, and Saturday." Suddenly she looked up at me and asked, "What day is today?"

I told her that it was Friday. She looked at me strangely and started singing the song again until I finally asked her to stop singing and go brush her teeth.

Because my husband normally fed them breakfast and dropped them off at the day-care facility, I figured that if I left the house by 7:45, I wouldn't be too late for work. After combing my daughter's hair and brushing my son's, I was ready to leave. I didn't even notice that my husband wasn't home until I went downstairs and he was nowhere to be found. Angrily, I fed the kids breakfast and hurried them into the van so I could drop them off. My daughter started singing the days of the week again. After singing she asked me again what day it was. I was so concerned about getting them to day care and getting to work on time that I ignored her.

As I drove to the day-care center, I heard my daughter singing that song again. Feeling stressed and frustrated and tired of hearing her song, I decided to call my husband to find out why he wasn't there to drop the children off. As soon as he answered the phone I started my inquiry, not giving him a chance to say anything. When he finally got my attention, he said something that surprised me. "Honey," he said, "it's Saturday. You don't work on the weekends."

I laughed so long and felt so foolish that I had no choice but to apologize to him. Out of the blue my wonderful four-year-old said, "Mommy, are you sure it's Friday? Because yesterday you said it was Friday, and Friday can't come two days in a week." I laughed and told her that Mommy had made a mistake and that today was Saturday.

She shook her head and said, "Silly Mommy. You must be tired."

As I turned around to head home, I looked back at my two-year-old son; he sat there sucking on his two middle fingers, looking very confused. He finally asked, "Why are we going home." I laughed as I listened to his sister tell him, "Because Mommy doesn't know her days of the week."

Crystal Davis

7

A MATTER OF PERSPECTIVE

The grand essentials of happiness are: something to do, something to love, and something to hope for.

Allan K. Chalmers

Eight Days a Week

We must not allow the clock and the calendar
to blind us to the fact that each moment of life is
a miracle and mystery.

H. G. Wells

The incessant rain kept me indoors, giving me a rare opportunity to finally clean out the closet in an upstairs bedroom. On one of the shelves, I found some old calendars I had kept from when my two boys were much, much younger. Removing clothes that were destined never to make it into my eighteen-year-old son's dresser or the hamper, I sat down on a chair in his room and perused the happenings of a year long ago. Thumbing through the entries from each of the jam-packed months brought back that incredibly busy time as if it were only yesterday.

No matter the season, the tiny box allotted to each day of the month was never big enough to contain the myriad jottings of appointments and reminders of important events, such as teacher conferences, dental visits, playdates, chess lessons, birthday parties, school plays, soccer practices, spring concerts, baseball games, class trips, day-camp field days, and Cub Scout bowl-o-rees. My Palmer-perfect penmanship went out the window those days because I needed to cram more into each day's tiny little square than often seemed humanly possible. Not listed on the calendar were the other important day-to-day events that were part and parcel of rearing two children—the 365 days of meals, laundry, baths, and bedtime stories.

As I sat reminiscing, I clearly recalled that in the midst of the whirlwind of rearing two sons, it often felt as if I would never have a minute to myself. But as hard as it was to savor every moment when they were young—especially when the control button on my body seemed to be stuck in "Fast Forward"—I knew the day would come when I actually would have the time to nurture my garden, read a good book, have a quiet dinner with my husband, and watch a movie that wasn't restricted to General Audiences.

The boys are older now, and we still have a family calendar, but it's a lot less crowded these days. My sons no longer need to be driven to three athletic fields in one day. Neither my husband nor I need to save a vacation day from work to chaperone a trip to the Metropolitan Museum or Big Apple Circus. And events with my children's now-grown childhood friends don't need to be inked on to the master calendar; at this age the "children" are more than capable of handling most of the day-to-day details of their lives on their own.

So for now I'm enjoying this respite on the calendar. Although my sons may someday keep their own family calendars on computers—where the boxes for each day can expand infinitely—I'm sure that one day I'll be asked, "Mom, can you check your calendar to see if you can babysit next Saturday night?"

I'm keeping the date open.

Pamela Hackett Hobson

Shortcuts and Illusions

The other day my daughter Cindy and I were having one of those blessed telephone conversations that helps us both span the too many miles between our family home in California and hers in Utah. She is a working mother of four children, ranging from ages nine to eighteen. And for anyone who juggles work, family, and home, or has done it, I needn't say another word.

"How did you do it?" she asked, forgetting for the moment that I had had only two children—not for a moment to minimize the accomplishment of that. It took everything I had and simply renders me in awe of those who do work, rear several children, and take care of the household. "You used to make us homemade doughnuts for breakfast on the weekends. Oh, how we loved those doughnuts. We would roll 'em in cinnamon and sugar and we'd glaze some." Her voice trailed off. "We were the envy of the neighborhood."

The happiness of the memory was apparent. A flood of warmth rolled over and through me, and I was pretty sure she was experiencing the same thing. My tendency in those days had been to feel that there was never enough mama to go around and that surely I could be or should be doing a better job. But here was my daughter, now a remarkably accomplished working mother herself, remembering something lovely from her childhood.

"I have a confession to make," I ventured with consternation. "I hadn't a hint that you thought they were homemade. Those doughnuts weren't made from scratch. That was a shortcut and an illusion."

"They weren't homemade?" Disbelief filled her voice.

"Actually, they were refrigerator biscuits that I cut the middle out so we could make doughnut holes."

"The holes were the best part," she said with a sudden smile in her voice that I couldn't miss. Then her tone sobered again. "But I can't believe they weren't homemade, Mom. I could have sworn you made them from scratch."

For a moment I saw her at age four, an adorable little pixie looking up at me with shining green eyes full of trust and love and delight and a sparkle all her own. "It's true, honey. That was back in the day when everyone had her own deep fat fryer. Couldn't get away with that now."

Words eluded us both for a few moments. "We had a lot of fun on those mornings," she said. "The kitchen smelled like a bakery. And the doughnuts were so warm and yummy. Making them always felt like the beginning of a special day."

She paused, and I could almost see the pictures in her head and the unexpected gratitude I felt for shortcuts and illusions. *Thanks, Spirit,* I breathed in silence.

"You know another thing you did that I always liked? In fact, I still do it with our family just like we used to when I was little. Everyone thinks it's a treat."

"I can't wait to hear." I prompted, eager to learn.

"How on Sunday evenings we used to make popcorn and have sliced apples and watch television together. Now we do that when we watch a family video. Everybody loves those evenings."

"It's great knowing something so simple can become a tradition and bring so many feel-good memories with it. I'm glad you told me." A feeling of immense blessing welled up in me again.

In both the memories that my daughter had shared with me, the ingredients couldn't have been simpler. Thank heaven for *love*, for it transforms all things, even shortcuts and illusions.

Jane Elsdon

Dog Days

I don't know what month Cain killed Abel, but I am willing to bet money that it was August. If, as T. S. Eliot wrote, "April is the cruelest month . . . mixing memory and desire . . . ," then August is surely the longest, draggiest, whiniest, most quarrelsome and disagreeable month, mixing boredom and discontent. All the shine has worn off what in June seemed so exciting and fun. Children who were in their swimsuits and flip flops by 6:30 AM that first week after school let out for the summer, jumping up and down, asking every five minutes what time the pool opened, now whine, "Do we have to go swimming?"

Nobody cares if they ever eat another bite of watermelon in their lives. The same boys who were up at dawn each morning raring to go, who could be seen only as quick brown blurs from the corner of your eye, bicycle centaurs, barely able to hold still long enough to bolt down a PB and J, in August wake at noon, sluggish and morose. They drape themselves over the furniture, staring blankly for hours at Popeye cartoons that their grandmothers watched when *they* were young girls.

Nothing is fun; nothing tastes good; siblings hate each other. "*Mom!* He is *so stupid!* He thinks that zzzzz should xxxxx with the kkkkk to kill the wwww! Why did you even have him in the first place?*He is so stupid!*" As if, when presented with a brand-new little bundle of pink and white baby swaddled in a soft blanket, I might have looked into Baby's face and then in horror at the nurse. "Oh no! Take this one back! You can tell just by looking at him that he will think he can use a Whatsit to stun the Zorgoff, when everyone knows you have to get the Key first! Take him away. He's going to be so *stupid!*"

Everything was beautiful in June. There were days and weeks and months to look forward to, filled with the prospect of camp and cookouts and fireworks. Endless marshmallows. Fish sticking their slick heads up out of glistening water and grinning toothlessly, saying, "Pretty please, catch me. I'm here, I'm yours, and I have a thousand million brothers." Miles and miles of uncharted territory to explore, depths to plunge, and adventure around every corner. There was buried treasure out there somewhere and the possibility it could be found by a boy who was smart enough and brave enough and didn't have to come in until 10:00 PM.

That was June. This is August. It is hot and muggy. Whatever treasure might have been glimmering in a cool, dark place then has certainly dissolved and rotted in the heat by now. Been eaten by dogs. Anyway, gone, and if not gone, then not worth the trouble. Nothing is worth the trouble. And isn't there anything good to eat? Sheesh!

As far as I am concerned, school cannot start soon enough.

You know that summer is well and truly over, no matter what the calendar might say, when Boy number one innocently sticks his foot out while taking out the trash, stretching perhaps, or imagining that he would someday earn a place in a modern dance troupe, and Boy number two (the *stupid* one) runs into it. Because he's, well, you know. It's not Boy number one's fault. He was just, you know, sticking out his foot. The last thing he wants in the world is to hurt anybody, even somebody *too stupid to watch where he's going!* Damnit. Huh? No way, Mom! That's cussing! Cussing is just as bad as hurting *stupid people.* Bed? Maaahhhh-uuuum! It isn't even dark yet!

Sheesh!

So good-bye summer! Hello school! I will pay any amount for pre-worn-out-looking cargo pants and Chucks, buy any number of three-ring binders, pocket folders, boxes of Kleenex, and bottles of hand sanitizer. I will agree to chair any committee, sell any number of raffle tickets, do anything, say anything. I will personally buy nine hundred pounds of chocolate and eat it standing on my head. Just let August be over. Soon.

Elizabeth Bussey Sowdal

Learning to Fly

How blessings brighten as they take their flight

Edward Young

I had finally finished another term of graduate school, and my job at the school district had just ended. My stressful journey to becoming a teacher had been taking a toll on me. For the first time in a year, I had free time on my hands. I had a whole month to relax, catch up on home projects, and hang out with my kids.

I found myself falling into a strange routine of lounging on the couch, channel surfing. My family had been tucked away for the night, but I lay awake flipping through the endless sea of infomercials, home shopping channels, and taking a tour of the late night comedy circuit. Sadly, nothing made me laugh or smile. I would love to blame my problem on insomnia, but that wasn't the case. My dog looked at me with pity. My body gave me all the signals that it was ready for bed, yet I ignored them. Why did I force myself to stay up so late? Why did I prolong the day?

I think that I was putting off the inevitable: I didn't

want tomorrow to come too soon. It would mean I had lost another day of my vacation and moved one step closer to going back to work and school. It also meant that I could avoid the morning wake-up call from my children and not face another day's to-do list. I had lost that spark that keeps us all eager to embrace each day that life gives us. I gave myself a pep talk, but I couldn't figure out how to get out of this funk. Eventually, I gave up, turned in for the night, and fell asleep.

Bright and blurry the next morning, my five-year-old son nudged me to wake up. Still half asleep, I looked into his adorable blue eyes and sweet face. Then I rolled over and told him grumpily that it was too early and to go back to bed. He obediently went back to his room, but returned like clockwork about twenty minutes later. We continued this song and dance for another hour. Each time I became a little more irritable and desperate for sleep. And each time he became a little more persistent to get my attention. I heard my toddler daughter coming to life in the next room and realized that my morning needed to start. Deep down I knew that my fatigue was my own fault for staying up too late the night before, yet I couldn't break the pattern. Finally, I dragged myself out of bed and went about my day.

Most mornings I walked around in a fog while making my kids' breakfast. Their chatter was a bit like listening to the birds chirping outside. A morning wasn't the same without it. However, one morning, my son asked me to read him a particular story in bed. I had written it for a graduate class. Because my son would be starting kindergarten in the fall, I had written about his first day of school. The book held a lot of sentimental value already, so I didn't mind forcing myself to open my eyes. To my amazement, my son did something that gave me the true wake-up call I needed. As we lay together in bed, I read him the final lines of the story:

> *On your first day of school*
> *You squeeze my hand tight*
> *And give me a great big hug*
> *Telling me you'll be all right*
> *That sparkle in your eyes*
> *Says you are ready to say good-bye*
> *And I let go of your wings*
> *And trust that you know how to fly*

Now, my son's five-year-old logic kicked in and he jumped onto the bed. Unable to comprehend the metaphor in the story, he simply asked me watch him try to fly. He proceeded to jump up and down on my bed while flapping his wings. His hopeful eyes and eager smile permeated every part of my soul. My heavy heart now felt light as a feather. I got up on the bed, and together we bounced up and down in a futile effort to take off. We landed in a heap and giggled. In that moment, I let all the stress of the last year melt away as my son reminded me that I had forgotten how to laugh.

With renewed energy, I grabbed my son's hand, and we went to wake up his sister. As usual, we found that she had turned her bed into a playground. She had surrounded herself with a sea of dolls, stuffed animals, and any other toy she could find. I sat down with my two babes in toyland and gave them a great big hug.

They finally let me go from their hugs. They had just taught me how to fly.

Britt Prince

"Our teacher has children! She's two-timing us!"

Hugs and Kisses

I have to confess that most days I like being a working mom. I like contributing to my family's financial stability, my company's success, and perhaps most important, to my own sanity. I like that my work conversations don't include knock-knock jokes and that disagreements usually end without the statement, "You're a poopy head."

At least most of the time.

But there are days when I don't like working. There aren't many working moms in my suburban neighborhood, and even fewer single working moms like me. Some mornings I drive by the stay-at-home mothers waiting at the bus stops with their children. They laugh at one another's jokes and their children's antics and sip steaming coffee from mugs. They look content, as if they could wait there forever. I know this isn't true, but some days I feel frazzled and envious as I drive past them.

This year, February 14 started as one of those days.

I had volunteered to help plan my daughter's Valentine's Day party. It would be my first experience helping in the classroom, a more visible role than my usual job of cutting and stapling papers for the teacher late at night or on my lunch break. As a member of the

Valentine party team, my job was to entertain and delight twenty kindergartners with crafts, snacks, and fun.

First step: the planning.

"Hi, Susan," my answering machine chirped one evening. "This is Party Mom Number One. We're meeting at the school cafeteria next Tuesday at nine thirty to make our plans. I know you work, but I hope you can make it."

Great. By 9:30 most mornings, I was typically well into an inbox of e-mails and my third cup of cheap coffee. But darned if I was going to miss *this* meeting.

The next Tuesday, I was greeted in the cafeteria by the three other moms on the party team. *This won't be so hard,* I thought, climbing awkwardly over the bench in my tailored skirt. Party Mom Number Two surveyed my suit, pantyhose, and heels. "Oh, right. You're our working mom," she said with a smile.

Right.

It was clear that the Party Moms had planned elaborate, kid-friendly gatherings before, complete with decadent treats, exciting games, and homespun crafts and décor that would make Martha Stewart proud.

My form of entertaining, on the other hand, was more like Lucille Ball in a lost episode of *I Love Lucy.*

I listened to the Party Moms rattle off their ideas, while I kept my craft and game suggestions, printed off the Internet the night before, tucked inside my briefcase.

For the most part, I kept quiet.

When the meeting was almost over and the others had selected what they would bring, I spoke up. "Let me bring the candy!" I blurted out. The Party Moms turned and stared at me. "For the game prizes," I added hesitantly.

"Perfect," Party Mom Number Three said. "We can always use candy. And we know you work."

The evening before the big day, I stopped at the store on my way home, tired and grouchy. I scrounged through the picked-over shelves and placed my two small bags of candy in front of the cashier. I tried not to think of Party Mom Number One rigging up her karaoke machine and burning a custom CD. Or Party Mom Number Two stocking her wheeled cart of craft supplies.

Never mind that Party Mom Number Three was baking a tower of heart cookies from scratch at that very moment.

The next morning, my daughter and I drove past the moms and children at the bus stops. I felt frazzled and envious and inadequate all the way to school. I prayed the hours would go by quickly—that is, until I heard my daughter as she skipped into the classroom.

"This is my mom!" she exclaimed. "She's here for our party." My daughter pointed excitedly to the bags in my hands. "And we have candy!"

I realized then, although I hadn't brought the heart-shaped boxes to decorate or the songs to play, I was a Party Mom, too, dressed in jeans and a red sweater like the others. Together, we moms laughed and muddled through the next two hours of helping little fingers to paint and little feet to dance. I felt as if I could stay there forever.

And I must confess that there was one advantage to being the working mom on Valentine's Day: I was the one who got to bring the Hugs and Kisses.

Susan Courtad

Reprinted by permission of Jonny Hawkins. © *1999 Jonny Hawkins.*

The New Age To-Do List

Thinking about all that needs to be done in the course of a regular day once left me feeling overwhelmed and unfulfilled. It was difficult to keep a positive attitude when faced with a to-do list filled with tasks, none of which came close to sounding like fun or seemed meaningful.

I struggled with a way to glorify the laundry pile, the grocery shopping, the eight hours in my office, and making dinner at the end of the day. No matter how I arranged the list, it still seemed like my day was filled with the mundane. I needed to bring a fresh outlook to my routine to readily accept the nagging list hanging on the magnetic notepad on my refrigerator.

The word *gratitude* came to mind as part of the solution to my to-do list dilemma. I decided to work with it, since I had no better ideas. I rewrote my list in an effort to make each task sound more interesting. Perhaps I could lure myself into feeling good about all that I needed to accomplish during a typically routine day.

It was surprisingly easily to transform the mundane into the enlightening, once I put my mind to it. With just one attempt, this is what I was able to come up with:

Typical To-Do List for an Ordinary Day in the Life of a Full-Time Working Mother

Old List–New List

Pay the bills—Compensate those who have provided goods or services that allow you to live as comfortably as possible.

Work in office—Utilize your mind, while providing your employer with the highest quality of work possible toward achieving common goals, as an exchange for monetary compensation.

Grocery shopping—Enjoy the abundance that life around you has to offer. Strive to provide a healthy and interesting diet for you and your family.

Clean the house—Create and maintain an inviting and comfortable environment, which surrounds you and your family every day.

Pick up child from school—Assist in the celebration of the end of another successful day at school. Embrace the opportunity to reflect on the day with your child while driving home.

Laundry—I'm stuck on this one. If you have an idea on how I might be able to look at this one in a positive manner please contact me ASAP, because my laundry is piling up as you read on.

Exercise—Enjoy the gifts of good health and strive to maintain it. Recognize that as long as you are on the treadmill, you do not have to do any of the other tasks on your list.

Make dinner—Celebrate the opportunity to provide proper nutrition for you and your family.

Clean up after dinner—I could say something about

creating the nice environment again, but in all honesty, I think just knowing that this is the last thing on the list for the day is good enough.

The new version uses more words, but it sounds a lot more meaningful. It has taken time to retrain my brain to accept the new descriptions that I have assigned to my daily routine tasks. If nothing else, the new list makes me smile with acknowledgment at what great lengths I have gone to remain optimistic about everyday life. Part of me does wish that I could have reworded at least one thing to sound like relaxing on a tropical beach far away from distraction. Knowing that the list is never-ending allows me to hang on to the promise that perhaps I will get a chance to work on my tropical beach in sometime in the future.

Shirley Warren

Balancing

It was Friday afternoon, and the longer than usual work week at my school had taken its toll. As I watched my daughters play in the neighbor's front yard, I was trying to stay awake until their bedtime. Betsy, my neighbor's daughter who was home for a weekend visit from college, kept me company while waiting for her girlfriends to pick her up for a night on the town. Soon our conversation drifted to one of the few things we had in common—an interest in teaching. Betsy was still unsure of her major, but leaning toward education.

"Balancing children and a career is really easy these days," said my young, unmarried, childless, unemployed friend. "It's especially true in the field of education with its child-oriented work schedule—not like going to an office or anything. It must be perfect for a single mom like you."

I had a vague memory of similar, naïve statements coming from my own mouth before marriage, children, or employment, so I tried to bite my tongue. "I can see how you might think that, having never experienced it firsthand," I said, knowing that she was right, up to a point. "It works smoothly as long as everything else in your life is running smoothly, which just doesn't happen all that often, at least not for me."

Her brow wrinkled with incomprehension.

"A sick child, a dead battery, or a visiting relative can wreck the best laid schedules quicker than the dog can eat a homework assignment," I explained. *Not to mention the inevitable students like Rusty with behavior problems, the likes of which they never tell you about in college,* I thought to myself. *They are the ones who keep you awake at night and take the time and energy of four of their peers.*

Betsy looked at me strangely.

"Really," she murmured, examining her fresh manicure, obviously losing interest. She made a move to leave, but I pinned her verbally to the lawn chair. I needed to vent, and before she decided on a major, she needed to hear the story of the underwear disaster.

"This week started out pretty well," I began. "A rescheduled ball game, a last minute birthday invitation, and an emergency run to the vet; the usual. Monday's afternoon faculty meeting lasted longer than usual, and I stayed late on Tuesday for a particularly unsatisfying conference with Rusty's parents. Wednesday night I was back at school for the PTA meeting."

Betsy squirmed and looked down the street for her friends. I figured I'd better get on with my story.

On Thursday the washing machine I'd bought at a garage sale during my own distant college years finally expired. I was behind on the laundry, but on Friday morning, I'd scrounged enough clean clothes together to get the children through the day. I then found a nice pair of navy slacks I hadn't worn in a while that happened to look great with my new green sweater. Things were clicking along until I opened my underwear drawer. There was not a pair of underpants to be seen! The idea of stuffing myself into my daughter's child-size undies was actually crossing my mind when a flash of color caught my eye. It was the pair of panties my daughters had given me for Valentine's

Day. They were lime green with large hot-pink hearts, white daisies, and orange bears scattered all over.

I encased myself in hearts, flowers, and bears, grateful but astonished that anyone would make such ridiculous underwear for an adult. I hurried to the car, where my girls were patiently waiting. I slid behind the wheel and heard the unmistakable rip of a plastic zipper.

I looked down to a sea of hearts and bears and flowers. Racing back into the house, I found a pair of white slacks that also looked perfect with my sweater. It was a little early in the year for white, but what the heck. That's the nice thing about second graders—they love you for who you are, not what you wear, right?

I got the carpool delivered on time and was just a few minutes late to my own classroom. When I arrived, all the students except Rusty were seated in their desks. He was seated at my desk, thumbing through my grade book, pretending to read everyone's name and giving them all Fs in every subject. One little girl already had tears in her eyes.

As the bell rang, I escorted Rusty to his seat and gently reprimanded him, using a week's worth of patience in the first five minutes of the day.

I was almost back to my desk when I heard a snort—unmistakably Rusty's."

"I can see the teacher's underpants!" he yelled.

The other children gasped, then craned their little necks to get a better view. They started to giggle. Soon the room was filled with uncontrollable laughter. I looked down, and sure enough, my wild panties were plainly visible through my white slacks.

The day went downhill from there as word spread like wildfire, and students from other classes made excuses to sneak a peek at the offending undies. It was so disruptive that when my break finally came, the principal sent me home to change. Of course, there was nothing to change into at home, so I headed to the mall where, in the space of thirty minutes, I bought a package of very respectable beige, no-pantyline briefs and a new washing machine— free delivery on Saturday.

My naïve, young neighbor was laughing as a car full of girls pulled up out front. My day-in-the-life-of-a-working-mom story had gotten her attention, but alas, not her empathy.

"I've decided to major in education," she cried, hurrying to meet her friends. "It sounds like such fun!"

I shook my tired head at the folly of youth, but you know what? She's right.

Margaret P. Cunningham

The Little Computer That Wouldn't

Working at home seemed like the perfect solution: no overhead, no commute. All I needed was a computer. I didn't bargain for a computer with a high-maintenance personality and a constant need for new accessories. I named her Barbie.

Barbie has been a challenge. Like all girls, she needs support that is both technical and uplifting. I've given her aromatherapy and astrology readings to soothe her. She loves to shop and wants—no needs—frequent additions to her software closet, even though I have outfitted her with a tasteful selection of lounge ware, casual ware, scan ware, and photo ware for all occasions.

She's temperamental. I don't know what she says to them, but I keep downloading new drivers and their licenses for her because she just can't hang on to good help. I've added the obligatory sacrificial RAM, a floppy drip drive, a modem in the latest colors and, after I got a burn permit from the fire department, a racy CD burner. To brighten her décor, I installed extra USB (Ultra Special Barbie) ports when she demanded and even threw in a pair of ethernet stockings.

Though born just last year, Barbie obsesses about her fading youth.

"Highly compensated engineers worked feverishly around the clock to program my irrevocable death precisely one day after my warranty expires," she moans.

"I know, I know," I say, "but don't worry, I've gotten your sagging warranty lifted three times already."

To relax, my sweet little computer has "developed" a penchant for pornography. I turn my back for a minute and she's bringing home smutty photographs. Man, has she got a thing for male enlargement products.

Occasionally, Barbie goes on strike. I think she was just agitating for a new living room couch when her fan started buzzing. I freshened up her inner spaces with air in a can to clean out the cobwebs, dust, cracker crumbs, and nacho cheese that had mysteriously accumulated. Barbie's fan whirred happily for a while, but in a fit of pique, she sputtered something about not feeling like it. That's when the good swift kick I learned from my mechanical dad came in handy (hey, it worked on the lawnmower). I kicked, and the fan shut up, an awkward but effective arrangement.

Last month, though, Barbie couldn't get her boots on in the morning without help. One day I turned her on and the screen was covered with exclamation marks, so I loaded her up in my car and took her over to our local computer geek shop.

I think Barbie was just starved for male attention because she booted up prettily for those guys, purring demurely and flashing her best screensavers.

"You got a power problem." They prognosticated. "You need one of these $300 batteries."

Barbie winked at me from the workbench.

Back home I plugged her into the hugely heavy, artificially enlarged battery reclining at her side. Still, she wasn't happy and refused to put on her boots, so it was back to the ER for Barbie and her jilted Ken.

"She needs a whole new wardrobe," the guys said. "A

fashion upgrade. She's hopelessly retro." Barbie's screen brightened as I left her with the high priests of the latest trends.

"She's running beautifully," they said when I returned. But as soon as Barbie got home, she refused to boot up. I was mad as I hauled her back to the boy's club.

"It's probably her mother-in-law board," they said this time.

"But she isn't married," I complained.

"Well, she's been corrupted," they said, shaking their heads sadly. "She works fine here. Why don't you sell her and get a new one."

After all I'd done for her, Barbie just wanted nicer digs. I thanked the guys but said no. In my opinion, Barbie needed an attitude adjustment.

I took her home. She wouldn't boot up, though I threatened to remove her modem privileges. A few days later when she was balking instead of booting, I didn't kick her but stroked her, whispering kind and supportive words into her side vents. I also placed a candy bar on her CD tray, thinking when the stick doesn't work, maybe a carrot is better.

She has worked perfectly ever since.

"Just a coincidence," the computer gurus said, but I know better. Sometimes, you have to give uppity girls like Barbie their due, and sometimes, flattery really will get you somewhere.

Carol Mell

"Can you call back next week? Our computer is down."

Real Summers

My kids have been out of school a total of two days, but already it's obvious—this summer will be the season they officially drive me crazy.

I don't know why it's so hard for them to comprehend the simple, sorry truth: just because they're off doesn't mean I am. Of course, I escape to the sanctity of my office cubicle each morning, which just means they know exactly where to find me.

"Hey, Mom, can you give me a ride to the bait shop?" Sean will ask. This is his eighteenth call of the day, and my morning coffee hasn't even cooled yet.

"I'm at work, son," I'll remind him. (When he dialed the phone, did he think he was calling our laundry room?)

"But you're coming home for lunch, right? What were you planning to do on your lunch?"

"Er, eat lunch?" Apparently the obvious answers elude this child. Or maybe I'm no longer spending time creatively.

I understand his excitement; no, really, I do, even if it doesn't seem that way to the boy on the other end of the phone. After all, I used to have "real summers," too, summers that spread out before me, one carefree day after another, when my greatest concerns included practicing "walking the doggie" with my blue Duncan Imperial or saving enough money to buy a cone when Mr. Softie rounded Red Bank and came down Frances. Alarm clocks were forgotten—stored away even—and teachers and homework were things of the past. For ninety-something days, I had to answer to only two bosses: the streetlight (since I had to be home before it was lit) or my mother's voice calling me home for dinner.

But ninety-something days aren't many, not really. So I can understand the urgency of getting to the bait shop on this, the second day of summer. After all, despite countless Beach Boys songs to the contrary, summers do end.

And in time, "real summers" end as well. Oh, sure, we still get the months of July and August, and those of us who are really lucky may even get a vacation, a week or two to abandon the production line or let the particulars pile up on the desk as we attempt to rest and recharge. That's a good thing—a very good thing—but it doesn't qualify as a "real summer."

"Real summer" can be understood only by kids, who know that the real start of the season isn't a date on the calendar. It's the ring of the dismissal bell on the last day of school. They fly out of the building, backpacks full of a year's worth of doodling, friends' phone numbers, and that summer reading list (which won't be glanced at until sometime late in August).

The chant may be "no more teachers, no more books" but the truth is "no more long pants, no more alarm clocks." Until that bell sounds again in September, my kids will fill their days catching fireflies and frogs, casting lures into the creek, collecting freckles in the sunshine, and sleeping well into morning after a long game of jailbreak the night before.

I heard my son sigh his impatience from the other end

of the phone, and suddenly I understood his annoyance. The truth: I was jealous.

I miss "real summers." Summers with alarm clocks are sort of like Christmas after your big brother spills the beans about Santa. Sure, the sun still shines, the sprinklers still flow, and Mr. Softie still rounds the corner. But it's not the same.

Remembering my own days of Popsicles and swim club, I agreed to spend my lunchtime picking up crickets and a container of worms. And, yes, the calls and distractions do drive me crazy, but I know that my boys are answering to their own summer bosses—the lure of a creek filled with catfish, the flitting dance of lightening bugs chased through freshly mowed grass, the summer refrain of childhood as it turns from sunlight to shadow one last time.

Knowing I'll never hear that song again drives me craziest of all.

Mary Dixon Lebeau

8

INSIGHTS AND LESSONS
The Joys of Work and the Secret of Balance

One hundred years from now, it will not matter what my bank account was, how big my house was, or what kind of car I drove. But the world may be a little better, because I was important in the life of a child.

Forest Witcraft

A Lesson Learned
When Tying Shoelaces

For working mothers, getting children ready for school in the morning and doing so in a timely and reasonably calm manner is a daily "opportunity for growth." How many moms have arrived at the office with a jelly stain on their "dry clean only" dress from the peanut butter and jelly sandwich made for school lunch? In addition to making school lunches, they also pour juice, make coffee, take a quick look at the newspaper headlines, look for a missing sneaker, and supervise the packing of school bags. It is no wonder that working moms often feel like it's nearly lunchtime when they first walk into their workplace, having accomplished more in the first two hours of their day than their coworkers can ever imagine!

The beginning of some days are less than ideal. I shudder at the times I've dropped our oldest son off at elementary school wearing his favorite T-shirt for the third time that week, his hair sticking up and toothpaste on the corner of his mouth. As I lean out the car window, rubbing the toothpaste away (and comforting myself by noticing that at least he brushed his teeth), I realize that I've blown it again. We've had a minor disagreement in the car ride to school, no doubt fueled by the quick-paced schedule both my son and I have kept since we awoke that morning. I drive away from the school feeling guilty that our morning routine and conversation have not prepared him for the best start to the school day. My mother's intuition told me that the negative interaction with my son that morning impacted how his school day went. My instinct was verified in a workshop I recently attended. It's humbling for working moms to have their guilt confirmed by "scientific" research!

While I incur stresses such as these as a result of being a working mom, over the years I realize I've learned some lessons about myself, my children have learned lessons about themselves, and we've learned lessons about and from one another that we wouldn't have learned if I was a stay-at-home mom. Because starting the day with personal reflection and prayer as well as getting work-related paperwork completed and e-mails answered makes me a more effective college professor, I've learned I need to get up earlier to have enough time for these tasks. Because I need to be getting dressed and making lunches at the same time our oldest son needs to eat breakfast and get dressed, he has learned how to be more independent by pouring his cereal and choosing what clothes to wear (which explains why he sometimes wears the same T-shirt more than once a week!). Because our oldest son likes to ease into the day by reading a book or leaning out the car window, while I like to talk when driving to school, we've learned to compromise during the twenty-five minute drive by having him spend half of our travel time reading and the other half talking about upcoming events of the day.

While these lessons have had a positive impact on me and my children, the most significant lesson I've learned while getting ready for work and school happened years ago when I was tying our oldest son's shoelaces for him before leaving for kindergarten.

I remember feeling pleased that we were running a few minutes ahead of schedule! Hurriedly tying his shoes, more out of habit than necessity, Colin put his hands on my shoulders and looked directly into my eyes. "Mom, why do you always have to tie my shoes so fast?"

I paused, and then responded, "I don't know, honey. That's a good question!"

In that brief exchange I learned more from my son about how to be a good parent than I could from reading countless books or attending workshops on effective parenting. My son taught me a lesson that has guided me through the years as he's grown from being a preschooler to a budding adolescent. People—not completing tasks—should be my focus as a parent. Live in the moment, appreciate each blessing, whether it be the fact that the start of our day has been relatively smooth or he has found a T-shirt or two that he likes to wear a lot!

Colin no longer needs me to tie his shoelaces; however, as I watch him put on his shoes each morning before we leave the house for school and work, I am reminded of this lesson he taught me years ago.

Margaret Haefner Berg

Are You Listening?

One recent morning, a morning like any other, I was involved in my usual assortment of tasks. I was preparing breakfast, getting the kids ready for school, helping my daughter finish some neglected homework, cleaning the kitchen, and all the while itching to get to the pile of e-mails and voice mails waiting for me in my office. I added one more task when I began reading a magazine article. The headline shouted: SOME ATTENTION MUST BE PAID!

While my daughter's sweet little voice prattled on about something I never quite heard, I proceeded to read the article. I read in my usual distracted fashion. I scanned a paragraph, realized I hadn't comprehended the words, then reread it. Scanned another paragraph, realized I hadn't comprehended it, reread it. Finally, it occurred to me what I was reading. It was an article about our distracted society. Carefully packing my car keys in my son's lunchbox, I read on.

Apparently, there was a gathering of technology types who talked about the advances in communications and business and what they mean for society. An executive stood to speak, and she identified an epidemic she called "continuous partial attention." As her audience ignored her to gaze into their laptops and check their phones for text messages, she elaborated.

She said that in today's world we are continually plugged in. Our mobile electronic devices keep us connected to all of our many responsibilities, no matter where we are. We live in perpetual contact with everyone and everything. We commend ourselves for our availability to those who might need us at any given moment, using tools always at our fingertips. Well, it's true! And don't you love it?

Thirteen years ago, when my husband and I decided to start a family, I knew that my high-pressure radio sales job would no longer suit my lifestyle. So during my seventh month of pregnancy with my first child, I put out the proverbial shingle and became a media-buying consultant. I brought with me some of the clients and contacts from my previous job, and I hit the ground running.

I knew that I had technology to thank for my ability to work from home. With faxes, voice mail, and the newly emerging Internet, work no longer needed to be done in "real time." I could communicate with clients and suppliers when it was most convenient for me. I could earn a good income for work I found enjoyable, while still being an available and attentive mother to my children. What a wonderful new world!

But thirteen years later as I stood reading this magazine, I realized that something had shifted. The article identified some alarming changes brought on by the new technologies. The proliferation of communication tools, such as cell phones, e-mail, and PDAs, has created a world in which our clients, friends, and acquaintances can contact us at any time or place. They can call us in our cars from their cars. They can send us texts asking us to take action. They can juggle two tasks at once by sending us an e-mail while talking to someone else on the telephone.

The balance has tipped. The fact that we now can be available wherever we are has evolved into the expectation that we *should* be available wherever we are. The pace of life has accelerated dramatically. And the result is that we're becoming more removed from the moment we're engaged in because we leave ourselves open to spontaneous interruptions that suddenly demand our focus. The technology that once expanded our time is now consuming it, leaving us constantly feeling like there's something else we're supposed to be doing.

Snapping back to the present, I realized that standing in my kitchen I wasn't particularly available to anyone! Noticing that my daughter had walked away from my lack of conversation, I suddenly wondered what it was she'd been trying to tell me. And how urgent were those e-mails in the other room at 7:30 in the morning when my kids were right there asking for just five more minutes of my attention? And what on earth was I doing reading a magazine article when the real task at hand was to get the children ready for school?

Well, it was one of life's little epiphanies. It reminded me of a lesson I keep relearning: the most worthy goal is to strive to be present and grounded in a tangible place and time. I had structured my life to be available to my clients when they needed me, but more important, to my children when they needed me. And that moment was now. The magazine and the e-mails and the voice mails and the cleaning could wait.

Contemporary life offers so many opportunities and choices for women, and each of us is figuring it out as we go along. I've discovered that while I have multiple responsibilities, each can be accomplished in its own time. I find it useful to block out sections of time for each of the things that matter, temporarily setting aside the rest.

There is something to be said for compartmentalizing, especially when our children are involved.

True, it does take a lot of practice to focus on being in the moment, but it makes life so much more meaningful. Distractions are everywhere, but our lives are now! No matter how much work we have to do—with careers, parenting, home maintenance, church, and civic involvement—if we put our whole minds and bodies into performing each task with intention, we can feel less burdened and more rewarded.

It is only when we pay attention to life as we're living it that the true richness of all we have can truly be appreciated. So let's never forget to seize the moment!

Jennifer L. White

Little Sounds

Work had piled up. I scooped the "Leaning Tower of Paperwork" off my desk. Underneath the mess poked a bright yellow envelope. Hmm, an unopened birthday card from my best friend. *When did that get there? My birthday was two months ago!* Studying the postmark, I realized the card had been mailed on time. I was the one who was late in opening it. I'd let it get buried under the mounds of paper and then had forgotten it.

Lately I'd been occupied with pressing projects, laundry, meals, my husband, Mike, and two kids (and let's not forget the dog!). I barely recognized anything less monumental than the sun rising and setting. I was too busy with *important* things. There just wasn't time to stop and notice the little things.

Like all moms, I'd been busy. But there was something I couldn't miss. My eight-month-old, Andy, seemed to be hurting. At night he'd wake up repeatedly, crying.

"What's the matter, little guy?" I asked one night, trying to soothe him back to sleep. Mike took a turn holding a bottle. But soothing and feeding didn't help. Andy cried and held his hand to his ear.

The next day, the doctor confirmed our suspicion. Andy

had a double ear infection. "He was probably born with ear infections," she commented. She started him on antibiotics. No sooner had he finished one course, though, than he got another infection. A few months later, the doctor scheduled him for a minor operation to insert drainage tubes in his ears. By the time he was three, he had to have another operation. I felt awful. In his short life, he'd practically never been without an ear infection.

The operation went smoothly. Andy soon came out of the anesthesia and was banging at the hospital bed rails, ready to break out of there. We bundled him up and took him home, along with a list of instructions and medicine.

That night I pulled the covers up under his little chin. "I was brave boy, right, Mommy?"

"Yes, you were very brave," I replied, kissing him good night.

"I love you all the way to Jupiter," he said, as he did every night.

"And I love you all the way back," I replied as usual, and flicked off the light.

We half expected Andy to wake up during the night as he had before, but he slept right through. The operation must have worked! For the first time in months, it seemed his little ears were pain-free.

But the next night, he woke up crying. *Oh, no, not again,* we thought, rushing into his room. "Andy, what's the matter?" I asked. "Do your ears hurt?"

Andy choked back his tears. "No, Mommy."

"Do you feel sick, then?" asked Mike.

"No, Daddy," Andy replied.

"Well, what could be the problem?" I sat on the edge of his bed and felt his forehead. It wasn't warm.

"I heard sumthin'," he said, eyes wide. We grew still, listening.

"That! That!" he said, frightened. We didn't hear anything.

"What's that *tick tick* sound?" He covered his head with his blanket.

Mike and I looked around the room and finally noticed something on his nightstand. "Andy, it's only your little blue alarm clock," Mike laughed. Andy peeked out from under the covers. "Haven't you ever heard that before?" "No," said Andy. We were amazed. His many ear infections must have affected his ability to hear softer sounds.

Later, Andy made more discoveries. For the first time he heard the swoosh his corduroy overalls made when he walked, the *huuummm* of the refrigerator's motor. Every day we reveled in his new discoveries. At night when I tucked him in, he giggled at the sound of his hair rustling against the pillow.

What a joy, I thought, *to be so delighted by something so simple.* That's the way I wanted to be! Looking at Andy, his eyes starting to droop, I made a resolution. Working or not, I wasn't going to be too busy to notice the little things anymore. Like the tick of a clock or the sound of my little boy's voice as he whispers, "I love you all the way to Jupiter."

Peggy Frezon

Mustaches on Cherubs

"I'm leaving you," said my husband. Moments before, he had taken me into the small study at the far end of our rambling farmhouse, away from the ears of our young son and daughter. I knew he had something important to tell me, but I didn't know it was earthshaking. "How will I ever support my children?" I wept uncontrollably.

As a stay-at-home mom, my life with the children had been storybook material. I loved the shrieks of young voices buried in heaped piles of autumn leaves, the whoosh of the horse-drawn sleigh packed with bundled kids in the falling snow, the race for the chocolate bunny hidden in the hollow of the old granny apple tree, the shouts of kids dangling from the large spreading chestnut branch.

Then three little words, "I'm leaving you," and everything changed. Moments of joy departed and mountains of work took their place. It seemed like things couldn't be worse, but I was to find out they could be.

Bloom where you are planted, I told myself. I put out the word that my farm was available for use. Neighbors came to board their horses in my barn stalls, and a horseback riding instructor arrived to teach in my split rail paddocks.

A young couple transformed my small cottage into their home, and eager townsfolk turned my enclosed pool into a swim club. The farm bustled with activity.

Relieved and grateful, albeit tired, I gathered up the checks from my tenants and paid my mortgage and bills.

Yet the challenges didn't stop. The wooden roof on my 1733 saltbox house leaked. The occasional drip quickly became a trickle.

Fortunately, my farmhouse was listed in the National Register of Historic Places, so I applied for a government grant. Workmen turned the drip, drip, drip of rain into the tap, tap, tap of hammers, and we were dry at last.

But cold. With little money for heating oil, summer turned into the winter of our discontent. When the kids and I put on a second layer of thermal underwear, it occurred to me that I own a forest out back. Why not use it?

I purchased a wood-burning stove on credit and found a state forester to mark our trees for cutting. A sharecropper split and stacked the wood. The kids and I carried in the logs. Cozy, cost-free heat soon filled the family-style kitchen. The grate I put in the corner of the ceiling allowed heat to drift up to the children's bedrooms. Perfect.

Encouraged by success, I pushed myself to the limit, picked blackberries, plucked Concord grapes, gathered apples, dug carrots, dried herbs, tapped maple sap, milked goats—labored thirty hours a week as a home care physical therapist.

Slow down, I heard an inner voice say. *Rest*—but I didn't, until a forest fire behind the horse barns got my attention. I raced top speed to the house phone, only to collapse on the threshold. Crawling to the receiver, I made two calls, one to the fire department and another to my doctor. Thankfully, the horses and barns were spared, but my heart took a terrible beating, literally. Diagnosed with arrhythmia, I was forced into the rest I had refused.

I wondered how I would ever pay the bills while flat on my back. But a peace came over me from who knew where, and I learned to meditate quietly. In the weeks that followed, the tenants' rental money still arrived, and the food stored up in my freezer and on my buttery shelf never ran out.

When my strength improved, I flung open the doors of the oak-beamed great room, previously used for festivities but closed to save heating expenses after my husband left. With a burst of extravagance, I piled our finest white birch logs into the spacious brick fireplace and set them crackling. Our collie shook fresh snow off his back and curled up by the warm blaze. Nestled in the large wing chair, with a child tucked under each arm, I read *Tales of Uncle Remus.* My lips contorted to capture the dialect, while the children squealed at the clever antics of Br'er Fox and Br'er Rabbit. Yellow candlelight flickered a message through the diamond-pane windows that all was well within.

Before bed, I gave each child a glass of rich chocolate milk. Dark brown mustaches incongruously painted themselves above pink cherub mouths and made me chuckle for the first time in months.

I became aware that work had possessed me. Mother Teresa said, "It is not how much you do but how much love you put into the doing that matters." Special moments with the kids again became my top priority.

As seasons passed, the kids and I responded when the drifting snow sighed for the old sleigh, when the granny apple tree flaunted her pink blossoms for a bouquet, when the swaying chestnut branch beckoned kids to climb, and when the swirling autumn leaves insisted we dance with them.

To my surprise, the work still got done, more easily than ever, and the expendable chores that were left undone were never even noticed.

Margaret Lang

Every Day Is a Good Day

Occasionally I hear on talk shows or among friends that age-old banter about what is best for young children: a stay-at-home mother or a full-time working mother. I have been on both sides of this argument, and the pros and cons of each have merit.

Without a doubt, leaving our three-year-old son, Mason, to head to work is not always easy. There are days when Mason is not sick but just not feeling emotionally up to preschool. When we have those days—which we all do—I struggle with wanting to call in sick and stay home with him, snuggle with him, revel in a play day with no stresses. Just "Mommy and Mason" time. But I don't. I get him ready for school and myself ready for work, and we head out the door.

I feel there is great value in teaching our children that we all have choices, and with those choices comes responsibility. I can choose to stay home with him, but he will miss out on valuable education and socialization, and I, in turn, will miss out on not only the accomplishments I achieve at work, but also providing a higher quality of life for our family.

I recently learned a valuable lesson about our perceptions of a stay-at-home mother versus a working mother. I rose early, knowing it was going to be a full day that would require precision scheduling. Unfortunately, Mason's preschool was closed for two presidential Monday holidays in a row; when this sort of scheduling conflict occurs, my husband, Dave, and I each take a Monday off. It was my turn to take Monday off, but I had to be at work. Besides holding a full-time outside sales job, I also have a nearly full-time real estate career. That Monday I had to be at my sales job, *plus* I had a full schedule of house showings for two separate families.

I reviewed my day closely and realized that I could schedule office time in the morning from home. I asked my dear friend and Mason's godmother, Dahlynn, to meet us at the local mall at noon sharp; Mason would get to have a special afternoon out with his "auntie." While he was with Dahlynn, I could make three scheduled sales calls. Timing was everything.

Like clockwork, Dahlynn met us at the mall. I whipped through my on-site sales calls across town and then returned to the mall for a quick lunch with Mason and his auntie, who had bought him a yellow helium balloon and a teddy bear for Valentine's Day. With kisses good-bye to his auntie, Mason and I stopped at the real estate office to pick up my listings and lock box key and then headed home to freshen up. We used the potty, combed our hair, and were out the door again in a matter of minutes.

The two of us showed several houses to my first set of clients. I was amazed to hear my three-year-old son showing the clients the size of the bedroom closets. After the showings to the first family, the plan was to race Mason home to have dinner with Dave, who would be home from work, and then I would leave again to meet the second family to show more houses.

On the trip home, I reviewed the day thus far. Guilt

slowly started to creep into my mind; was this all too much for him? A busy morning at home, dropping him at the mall, carting him to the real estate office and then to the showings—did he understand all of this running and going, going, going, or did he think his working mom was crazy?

We pulled into the driveway at the same time Dave was getting home from work. Before I could say a word or even begin to express my concerns about feeling guilty, Mason yelled to his dad from his car seat, "Daddy, Daddy! Mommy took me to play with Aunt Dahlynn and look what she bought for me for Balentine's Day, a bear, Daddy, a teddy bear, with a balloon, we played and looked at toys, and then Mommy came to have lunch with us, and then we went to see houses, and I helped Mommy at work with the houses, Daddy, it was the best, fun day ever!" He said all of this in one big, long breath, as only a three-year-old can do.

My guilt of being a busy working mom with two full-time jobs instantly subsided. I realized that regardless of my hectic schedule, Mason was truly happy. His running dialogue to his father taught me that he likes being a part of my day-to-day life, whether it's a very busy workday, a lazy Saturday, a good day, or even a bad day. But most important, Mason taught me that any day is a great day as long as we can be together.

Kathleen Partak

Moms Know Everything

It was a dark and rainy Wednesday when my parents woke me up. I felt as gloomy as the weather—I had a spelling quiz later that day. I was in first grade, and it was to be my first quiz ever. Did I really know all the words? Or was I clueless? I wasn't planning to find out.

The night before, I schemed what I thought was a perfectly mischievous plan, sure to fool both of my parents. As I sleepily opened my eyes, I let out a horrific groan. "Mommy," I whined, "my stomach hurts." I groaned once again to make sure that my mom had believed what I said.

"You have a stomachache?" my mother kindly asked, and I nodded with yet another moan. "Does it hurt anywhere else, honey?" my mother questioned me again, feeling my forehead.

"No, not right now," I replied.

My mother took my temperature as my father leaned over me with concern in his eyes. I was usually a very healthy child, and up-to-date on all my shots, so my parents pondered what could be wrong. The thermometer beeped, revealing that I did not have a fever. My mom looked from the thermometer to me and back again to the thermometer. I knew something clicked in her head. My mom knew that I had a spelling quiz that day and that I did not complain when I was sick. The thermometer signaled that I was okay, and I looked as healthy as ever.

With a twinkle in her eye, my mom instructed me to lift up my shirt so she could examine my tummy. *Just some stomach prodding and I'll be on my way to skipping school and that dreadful quiz,* I thought.

My mother gently poked my stomach and made knowing noises, "Hmm, umm, yes, yes." I couldn't take it any longer and let out a yelp of laughter, and was soon rolling around screaming with giggles as my mother proceeded to tickle me.

As I settled down, everyone knew my cover was blown and that I was not sick. I desperately insisted that I was in agony and then, knowing that was useless, started begging to stay home. My parents refused, and slowly I got dressed and ready for school.

Later that day, I found out that spelling quizzes weren't really monsters out to eat me, but soon-to-be familiar parts of my school days. Since then, I have never faked being sick because I haven't needed to. I also know that it is nearly impossible to fool my mom, a pediatrician, into believing that I am sick when I'm not. After all, moms know everything.

Emily Rider-Longmaid

Sick Day

I leaped out of bed—on the right side, of course—after eight hours of peaceful, uninterrupted sleep. I was ready to start the day. My daughter dressed herself without incident (meaning neither tears nor blood were shed, and no animals were hurt). My husband packed her a nutritious lunch and handed it to me, along with a pink backpack, as my daughter and I walked toward the door five minutes ahead of schedule.

"You look beautiful today," he said admiringly, as he planted a sweet kiss on my forehead.

He was right. I was ten pounds lighter and four inches taller in my sleek new suit. I was modern motherhood personified: a loving spouse, a brilliant child, a fulfilling career. I had it all, and I had it all under control.

I pondered the possibilities for world peace as I drove off with my smiling daughter for what would undoubtedly be another wonderful day and then—*What on earth was that god-awful sound?*

I realized I accidentally set the alarm instead of the radio. I reached for the greatest invention of the postmodern era: the snooze button.

The dial read 7:05 AM. How could it be? I had just

completed an emergency work assignment a few hours earlier and must have set the time incorrectly in my sleep-deprived stupor.

I had precisely thirty minutes to get my five-year-old ready for school and make myself presentable. Luckily, I had taught my husband how to dress himself years before.

"Wake up, Sarah," I cried into her room. "We're running late!"

I took a five-minute shower and threw on the first thing I saw. An ill-fitting sweater and granny skirt, a hair scrunchy and no makeup. Not exactly *Sex and the City*, but it would have to do. And why did my cell phone keep ringing? I wished I had taken the time to learn how to change the grating standard ring.

I went to check on my daughter, who was still lying in bed. I threw off the covers and threw on her uniform. No time for hair ribbons. No time for a complete and balanced breakfast. No time to notice the child's listless and warm body.

I dragged the little girl to the front door. My husband, still in his robe, rushed behind us with her backpack and jacket. Today would have to be a school lunch day.

It was 7:40, and there was still a chance we would make it to school on time. We didn't look our best but, in the sole resemblance to my fantasy, neither tears nor blood had been shed.

And then Sarah, who had been quietly standing at the door, threw up, clearly violating the sick ban I had imposed on the family when I went back to work full-time. It was more like a commandment: Thou shall not, under any circumstance, get sick. In the event that anyone dared defy this order, they were then prohibited from passing on said disease to any unsuspecting family members.

We abided by this law, and as a result had willed away

many a cold, cough, and sneeze. But we couldn't live in denial forever, especially when a kindergartner comprises one-third of the household.

By then I could see that Sarah was burning up. I tried to figure out what to do as I cleaned her up and put her back under the covers. Maybe I could take her to the office with me for a little bit. Or maybe my husband could cancel his appointments and stay home with her for part of the day.

And then Sarah threw up again, and it finally hit me. I wasn't going anywhere. My little girl needed me.

I had no Plan B for situations such as the last-minute stomach flu. There weren't any available grandparents or babysitters on speed dial. There was no friendly neighbor from whom to ask a big favor.

To make matters worse, there was neither an understanding boss nor forgiving clients in the picture. It was most unprofessional to stay home with a sick child. Advertising deadlines wait for no man, woman, or child.

I sat down at my laptop as my husband left for work, lugging a briefcase full of his own guilt. I wanted to call my boss, but I knew I wouldn't be able to bear his verbal disappointment.

I e-mailed him the reason for my unforeseen absence. His response was characteristically heartless: Please e-mail me the copy for the ads we discussed yesterday.

The cold harshness of the workplace does not allow "hope your daughter feels better" or any other sympathetic banter that does not result in increased company revenues. With Sarah in bed and the front hallway cleaned up, I figured I could probably get some work done from home. I scrolled through other e-mails from countless clients with countless requests who did not care that a sick child needed her mother.

Then it dawned on me. A sick day is a sick day. And my child is a part of me, an extension of myself; therefore, if she is sick, I am sick. I put the guilt aside and decided to be thankful that I was home nurturing my little girl's tummy ache rather than sitting by her side in a hospital room.

I e-mailed my boss the material he requested and forwarded client e-mails for coworkers to handle. They would have to do without me for a day or two, because my daughter did not have a back-up mommy.

And those barf-ridden sheets weren't going to wash themselves.

Brenda Rosales Rincon

Paving the Road
from Nanna to Mamma

If you find it in your heart to care for somebody else, you will have succeeded.

Maya Angelou

Elizabeth's call came from her daughter, Mary, who was in hysterics because her baby's father had been killed in a motorcycle accident. Always blaming others for her bad decisions, Mary had never outgrown her dependence on others for financial and emotional help, and she was not handling this situation very well, so Elizabeth quickly picked up two-and-one-half-year-old Jamie to allow Mary her space.

Within days Elizabeth learned that Jamie needed a safe harbor permanently. Justifying the gut-wrenching decision to take temporary custody, she asked a therapist friend for advice. "You can take custody now and have your daughter hate you forever. Or you can wait until—not if—something happens to Jamie, and then hate yourself forever."

The tranquil life Elizabeth and her husband, John, had known for ten years changed immediately as they became instant parents to a toddler. John became a quick study in the art of being a daddy for the first time in his life. The once quiet telephone rang constantly. Fear saw them sleep with the sheriff's home telephone number taped to their phone. Constant toddler noise prevented work, thought, and adult conversation. Late nights were reserved for talking and crying, until they fell into bed exhausted. Nap times were used to research the problems they were seeing with their daughter as they sought to understand how things went so wrong.

They also faced housing challenges. About the same time Jamie was born, Elizabeth and John had downsized to a small, rural cottage to create a memorable place for Jamie's visits. What was once the guest room became Jamie's room, toddler furniture replaced antiques, kiddie clothing was crammed into an already overflowing closet, with Barbie clothes underfoot, and hair scrunchies dominated the only bathroom.

Elizabeth became a rubber band stretched thin, and the mileage tripled on her now-too-small car. Schedules were changed without notice—a total loss of control. There were frustrating meetings with attorneys, work with a family counselor for advice from potty training to explaining death, and frequent out-of-town visits to Jamie's other grandparents. Without the loving support of friends and family to offer a shoulder and an ear, Elizabeth's seams would have burst during this tumultuous time.

Elizabeth and John won temporary custody in a second court battle after Mary was arrested for grand larceny and put on probation. Her behavior spiraled downward, and her emotionally draining attacks against her family escalated.

A year later, Elizabeth's stomach churned violently, preparing for the most important trial. There was total shock after Mary lost permanent custody of Jamie and was immediately arrested for probation violations. Instead of relief and celebration for winning permanent custody of little Jamie, Elizabeth stood sobbing at the image of her only child in handcuffs, going to prison.

Handling the overwhelming changes and the extra energy output of caring for a toddler was nothing short of a miracle for someone with chronic fatigue syndrome and fibromyalgia, but Elizabeth's determination served her well. She learned to relax more and to enjoy each day's journey, even declaring Tuesdays as "no shoes, no makeup day" to stay home and just be.

Elizabeth allowed her successful speaking business to slow down, and although she enjoyed speaking to hundreds, she now thrived on her dramatic stories to a captive audience of one little girl. She declined an opportunity to host an HGTV show, choosing instead to teach Jamie how to cook and garden. Turning down a publisher who wanted her to write a book, she took on a mission of writing articles to educate others about the alarming rise in grandparents rearing grandchildren. She began reaching out, and now she's not only paving the road from Nanna to Mamma in her own life, but also in the lives of others.

Her story is not rare. It happens frequently, because worries don't vanish when the kids are grown.

In the midst of the chaos that life threw her way, Elizabeth learned to accept that crises and crying fits are a part of life and that there's no reason to feel guilty or unsuccessful because of them. She also learned that the loving support of partners, family, and friends are worth their weight in gold. After searching many years, she found the definition of success: Believe in your ability to succeed and do the best with what life hands you one day at a time. When you reach out to others and have their best interests in mind, you gain strength, focus, and clarity in what you need to do with your life. When you help enough people succeed, you can't help but have some of that success rub off on you.

Pat Moore

Prioritize to Simplify Your Life

Do not race through life. Take the time to not only smell the roses, but watch them open.

Sharon McElroy

I am a working grandmother, and in looking back over the years, I wonder how I managed to do it all when my three children were an active part of my busy life. I believed in the traditional life—home-cooked meals; a clean home; a manicured yard; all clothes ironed, mended, and handmade; and being there for my family no matter what. But what this boiled down to was that I was over-worked and overwrought.

From my mother I learned that always being there for my family wasn't easy, and there was only so much of me to give, but out of love I found myself giving even more. Many days and nights I was drained and in need of at least eight hours of sleep to function normally. I could not fathom how I awakened after only five or six hours of sleep most nights.

At 4:30 AM the alarm would rudely blare. Slowly I would awaken and reluctantly rise from bed to quickly ready myself for eight hours at the office. I would then awaken my children, dress them or supervise them getting ready for school, pack lunches, prepare breakfast, eat, do the dishes, and off I would race to take them to school and to arrive at work on time by 8:00 AM. Not easy to do. With never enough time in the morning for me, often I found myself applying my makeup at each red light.

At 5:00 PM the race after the tiring workday started again. Sometimes I would need to stop at the grocery store before arriving home to cook dinner and complete or delegate chores. And too often there was homework to help with. After a long day in school, I don't believe children should be given homework. It is like taking your job home with you, and who enjoys that? After dinner, homework, baths, before you know it time has run out, and it is time for bed. And weekends? Usually those were spent completing chores that couldn't be finished during the week.

In retrospect, I recognize all the precious time lost in the hectic race of life because of its many responsibilities. Could I have slowed it down? Could I have simplified and balanced my life to become a calmer, happier person? Could I have made my loved ones happier? Yes. And over the years I finally learned how to do just that.

Still, I work full time at an office and part time writing and submitting whenever I can. I didn't back then, but now I enjoy time with my friends and loved ones. My life is very full, especially with the addition of four wonderful grandsons, but I don't race anymore. And I don't have to put makeup on at red lights any longer. I have learned to simplify my life by doing only what really matters. I changed my work schedule to avoid the dreadful 4:30 AM wake-up alarm. I let some unnecessary chores slide without feeling guilty, and I don't iron all the clothes. By not cooking, I don't waste time cleaning up the mess and thereby have leisure time to visit with friends or family at a restaurant and still enjoy a good meal. I create peaceful, enjoyable, quality time with my children, who are now grown and independent, and frequently I spend priceless time with my grandsons. No job, no race, is worth more.

Poet, singer, songwriter Rod McKuen wrote an insightful poem entitled *Age Is Better*. And I agree. I finally crossed the finish line, content in knowing that I have simplified my life by balancing responsibilities and accomplishing what brings the greatest happiness to myself and to others. My children will grow to learn this one day soon, I hope, and so, too, shall you. But why wait for precious years to pass? Why not prioritize, balance, and simplify your life now?

Sharon McElroy

The Road to Independence

This morning started out like any other except that by the time I finished packing my kids off for the day, I saw a piece of my daughter's girlhood vanish.

It all began as I bundled up my girls, Alison and Melissa, twin nine-year-olds, for day camp at the town pool. The girls were in their bathing suits when I turned to Melissa and asked her to put on her cover-up. Early in the season, I had purchased swim suits for the girls with matching cover-ups, but I noticed that neither twin was wearing them.

"Can I just wear a T-shirt, Mom?" asked Melissa, a bit nervous that I might be upset by the request.

"I thought the cover-up was cute," I answered. "I bought it to match your bathing suit."

Melissa locked on my eyes and smiled apologetically.

"Can I go now, Mom? Katie's here." And she skipped out the front door in an oversized T-shirt, courtesy of her big brother, Matt.

The T-shirt wasn't pretty, mind you, and it was neither expensive nor matched her bathing suit like the one I had bought. In fact, it was bordering on ratty.

But it was one thing the outfit I had purchased was not: it was cool.

"She just wants to be like Katie," Alison said. "She wears T-shirts over her bathing suit, like her older sisters. They're teenagers."

"What?" I asked.

Since when did my little girls want to be like anyone except, of course, me? Didn't the girls say they wanted to grow up and be writers like their mom? Didn't they pretend to be me, crunching their right shoulders to hold the phone, while using their free hands to do tasks around the house? Didn't they raid my closet regularly so they could try on my best dresses and my high heels?

Then it hit me. The moment long ago when being cool suddenly became important to me. It was around the same time that I stopped dragging out my own mother's 1940s-era silver trench coat that reminded me of Joan Crawford. It was when her once magical costume jewelry, the jewelry that transformed a ten-year-old me into a glamorous movie star, suddenly looked unfashionable and, well, old. I didn't want to be like my mom anymore. I wanted to be like Amy Burofsky, the cool girl at school with all the cute outfits.

Then I realized that it had been a while since I had been infuriated with the girls on a Saturday night because I couldn't find my other high heel. And I hadn't seen my closet looking like Macy's after a 70-percent-off sale for some time. The girls hadn't been rummaging in my closet.

When did it stop? When was the last time the girls helped me dress for an evening out when they would say, "Mommy, you look so beautiful." Now, Hillary Duff is the person they sigh over.

It is as it should be, of course. Children need to become independent of their mothers, don't they? I remember the countless times I dreamed of this moment, when I wished my girls were older and less dependent, so that I could have more time and freedom to do what I wanted to do—

to meet my deadlines, to go to the gym, to have a clean house. (Okay, so that's not going to happen yet!) I remember counting the minutes until my husband came home so I could run out to—anywhere—for a few brief hours of alone time. I remember times when I felt stuck, suffocated, invaded.

No, I'm not going to throw out some corny aphorism. Well-meaning people always throw out sage advice, such as "cherish the moment," during the worst possible moment, like a toddler meltdown at the supermarket. I hated those comments then, and I hate them now, too. I will never miss temper tantrums. And though I've missed out on some special moments because of my exasperation, there are so many other times when I delighted in my kids' childhoods and held those magical moments dear.

What the sages didn't say was that the child-rearing years are a little like being a teenager—you really can't comprehend what you have until after it's passed. It's only when you're thirty-five and long past all the tumult that you truly understand what all those parents meant when they said, "If only I knew then what I know now."

Now, I finally understand what a colleague was telling me years ago when she came to work one morning upset with her eight-year-old son, who had forgotten his lunch. She had raced after the school bus to catch him, and he was mortified, not because she wanted to give him his lunch, but because he said the flab on her legs wobbled as she ran.

At the time, I remember thinking she was being ridiculous and a bit vain. She was thin, and her son wasn't exactly the arbiter of good looks. After all, he was only eight.

Now, I finally understand that she wasn't crying about the wobbly flab on her legs. She was crying for her son's lost innocence. That day, as she ran to the bus, her son realized his mother was not the most beautiful woman in the world. She was his mother—and he still loved her, yes, but he saw her flaws.

That day she went from being Wonder Woman to being human.

And she didn't like it.

I don't blame her. Neither do I.

Pat Winters Lauro

Dandelions and My Little Samantha

Unless the rains came early, we did the same thing every workday morning for thirty-three mornings. First, we'd set up the stroller. Second, we'd load it up with a handful of animal crackers, a baby bottle of milk, and a one-year-old granddaughter. Next, we'd head out the front door to travel the mile from her house to my house. Then, as we'd slowly traverse the muggy Florida neighborhood, we'd gather dandelions growing in some of the lawns along the way.

What incredible joy these happy yellow weeds inspired in us! Samantha, my little princess, would squeal with delight whenever we saw a yellow flower bobbing in the distance, and I, a fifty-six-year-old English teacher on hiatus for the summer, would practically melt with happiness at the sight of this child awash in golden morning sunlight.

Samantha couldn't wait for me to place a fresh-picked stem into her hand, and by the time we arrived at our destination, she would have thoroughly examined, tasted, and eventually mauled many little flowers that we had collected along the way.

As the summer progressed, so did our discoveries. Soon we examined pinecones from the nearby trees, abandoned pennies left on the sidewalk, and bugs and snails that crossed our path. We learned to mimic birdsongs and to creep past magnificent white herons that often landed in yards to feast on the plentiful lizards and frogs.

The breezes were like heavenly kisses that cooled our warming faces. Even when it is still early in the day, the Florida heat becomes oppressive; that is why we really appreciated the pleasant shade of the magnolia tree that spread its huge canopy over my backyard.

· When we arrived at this, our destination, we had other things to discover—wind chimes that filled our air with soft sound, dirt and pots and flowers that needed to be put together by big and tiny hands, and kitty cats that just barely tolerated little girl investigations. Samantha enjoyed such adventure in this ordinary place under my adoring watch.

However, these wonderful activities had a bittersweet quality to them. I had been a working mother and felt that I had missed too many childhood miracles of my own children as I sought to put a roof over their heads and food in their stomachs. It is such a difficult dilemma for most women in the United States—in order to have children, you have to work, and in order to work, you let others spend the time with your children that you crave for yourself.

I remembered those bone-tired evenings when I came home and wanted only to plop down in front of the television so that I might rest a few minutes. I remember the guilt I felt that my children were getting only the "leftover me." What I didn't understand then was that children don't want lavish attention, expensive things, or extravagant vacations. All they really want is a small portion of time filled with meaningful interaction.

Dandelions, pinecones, or sugar maple burrs become childhood currency, and parents willing to rest outside in a lawn chair to watch children's games instead television, or parents willing get down on the living room floor to become a mountain to be crawled upon: these parents are a true treasure.

I have spent my adult life as a teacher of literature, and I suspect that is because my mother read to me every night before I went to sleep. *Winnie the Pooh, Mary Poppins, The Wizard of Oz, The Arabian Nights*: these were her legacy to me—these magical excursions into fantasy.

I read to my daughter when she was young, and she now reads to Samantha, even before this little soul could speak many words of her language. Something more than reading skills were transmitted across the generations, though. We were and are sharing time together, and this was and will be the "sticking place" in our hearts. This is the "tie that binds"—a memory of time shared that has shaped who we are and will shape who we will become.

Working parents simply need to make little special times happen whenever possible—a game of catch here, a romp through the sprinkler there, a game of hide-and-seek before supper, or a quilt tent-fort built in the dining room. These are the little moments that matter most to us in life. Just because they don't cost a fortune or take forever to prepare doesn't mean that they are unworthy, quite the contrary.

In the end, I bet it is the "dandelion moment" that will be my legacy to Samantha. It will be a subconscious thing, I would imagine. For some reason she will always have a tender feeling whenever she sees a summer morning with yards filled with yellow blossoms. And who knows? She might just want to become a botanist. In any case, she will have had these wonderful mornings with her grandmother, and that, as did "the road less traveled," may make all the difference.

Dorothy K. Fletcher

Fate and Hindsight

It was a Monday morning in the middle of winter. Snow had fallen a few days earlier, and although much of it had melted, the temperature outside was still below freezing. Not wanting to get my kids out in the icy muck, I wondered if school would be canceled. Yet I also fretted about the pile of work that would accumulate on my desk if I didn't make it to the office. When the television news anchor announced schools would be open, I took one last sip of coffee and walked back to my bedroom to decide what to wear.

Dressed, but sans makeup, I walked into my son Adam's room. He opened his dark brown eyes and smiled from his crib. "Hi, Mama." There was nothing sweeter than my baby's first smile of the morning.

My weekday morning dance carried me to my four-year-old daughter's room. Andi beamed like sunshine in the morning, her blue-green eyes clear and bright. "Time to wake up, sugar," I said softly.

I returned to my son's room to dress him. He jumped up and down when I approached his crib. This was always the best time of my day. No matter what struggles we encountered the night before—midnight cries, diaper changes, trips to the bathroom, or my tossing and turning with a little visitor in our bed—seeing my kids first thing each morning wiped the slate clean and started each day with a smile. My only question was how could days that had begun so sweetly turn so tense by the time we walked out the door?

"Andi! Come eat; we're going to be late!" I raised my voice again.

Adam was in his high chair, Cheerios dotting his face. I made lunches, while constantly monitoring the time. We were running behind, and I knew the process of getting coats, hats, gloves, lunches, backpacks, and diaper bag would add more delay to our departure.

My independent daughter struggled to get her coat on, and I bundled up Adam. They waited in the kitchen like little stuffed animals while I went to the garage to start the car. I returned to gather my little brood. With backpacks and lunches in one hand, and Adam on my opposite hip, we paraded to the car. I put Adam into his car seat and snapped him in, while Andi waited patiently in her booster seat, ready to be strapped in.

After shutting their door, I stood up, took a deep breath, and got into the car. My mind ticked down the daily list of what to bring with us. Got it all. Next, the day's to-do list. And first on my list: apologize to my captive audience for my loss of temper. I so wanted to be the perfect mom—like Mrs. Cleaver or Carol Brady—never losing my patience. But I'd failed again.

"I'm sorry I got mad at you," I said as calmly as my frazzled self could muster. "Mommy has to be at work on time, just like you have to be at school on time. You don't like to be late, do you?"

"No, Mommy," Andi answered. Adam mimicked his big sister.

"Well, neither do I." Did they understand?

The road was still slick in places. Seeing cars in ditches, I cautiously maneuvered the hills and curves of my neighborhood. The snow wasn't pretty now, just muddy and gray, with patches of brown grass showing through.

When we reached the freeway, I knew to be watchful of the black ice. Cars zipped past, driving at or above the speed limit. Tension weighed heavily on my shoulders, and my white-knuckled hands clutched the steering wheel. Oblivious to it all, Andi hummed a tune in the backseat, while Adam looked out the window and carried on his own conversation.

Squeeeeal . . . Hnnnk! Squealing tires followed by a loud thud shuddered through my bones. Rubber on asphalt and metal against metal. Looking in my rearview mirror, I was horrified to see a monster semitruck behind me, its huge grille pressed against the back window. The truck had pulled into my lane and hit the left rear bumper of my little Escort, knocking us in front of him.

Hot adrenaline surged through my body, while desperate thoughts flooded my mind. *My babies—God protect my babies. He's going to broadside us!*

Finally, we spun out of the path of the truck, but my car still whirled out of control across four lanes of oncoming traffic. Do I turn the wheel in the direction of the car's spin or against the spin? Black ice. Cars rushing to get somewhere on time. Tires screeched all around us, and I dreaded the inevitable bangs and crashes. I could only wait as the drama unfolded—spinning, spinning.

At last my car came to an abrupt stop on the other side of the freeway. Instinctively, I jerked my head around to the backseat, afraid of what I would see. Relief washed over me like a cooling stream. The precious sight of my babies' untouched bodies is forever etched in my mind's eye.

"Mommy, what was that?" Andi's eyes searched mine for assurance that everything was okay.

Then Adam smiled and said, "Do that again!"

I took a deep breath and laid my head on the steering wheel, my body trembling.

Fate sent us a miracle that morning, and for me it was a reality shift. Fate, like hindsight, can change how we see our lives, bringing what's important into clearer focus. Life is not perfect and neither are mothers. I'd spent too much time trying to live up to perfection and too little time appreciating the simple joys of my motherhood. I saw it clearly after that morning.

Jan Morrill

Back in the Saddle Again

Our son being diagnosed with juvenile diabetes had forced Charles and me to make some decisions and to reprioritize our lives. We decided that I would homeschool Wesley to allow us all the opportunity to adjust to the new demands of having a child with diabetes. Wesley and I spent his junior high school years together learning English, math, social studies, and science. As Wesley became ready for public high school, it was time for me to reenter the work force.

It was amazing how much the field of social work had changed in the three years I stayed home. I thought I had a pretty impressive resume. I had worked in residential services, foster care, and adoptions. I was shocked to discover that nobody wanted to hire a stay-at-home mom. Whenever I interviewed for a job and was asked about what I had been doing for the last three years, a stonelike expression would come over the interviewer's face, followed closely by, "I see you were homeschooling your child." The message was clear. Why hire a thirty-something stay-at-home mom with credentials and experience when they could hire a twenty-something, fresh out of school, with the same credentials?

The process of reentering the workforce became a daunting challenge. Interviews became the enemy. Frustrated, I applied for a job working with an adult population, although I had no previous experience working with adults. To my surprise I was not asked to go on a second interview; instead a few days after the initial interview, I was offered the position. Not only was I going back to work, but I was going to be a unit manager of a state-run facility that provided quality care for persons with mental disabilities.

I was given the task of supervising a staff of twelve, who made it quite clear that they did not want a new supervisor. Every time I requested that something be done, I was told, "Our old supervisor didn't do it that way—she did it this way." Thirty days into the job, I asked myself what stupidity had possessed me to take a job for which I had little experience. My office hours spilled over into my family time as my staff looked for any excuse to call or page me during my off hours. I was not a working mother; I was a frantic mother hanging on to my job by my chipped fingernails.

Fed up with the intrusion into my life, I prepared a letter of resignation. Before I had the opportunity to deliver it, we were sitting around the dinner table when I asked Wesley about his day in school. He looked at me and shrugged his shoulders before saying, "It's been difficult to adjust to being back in school. Some of the kids think I'm weird because I have to go to the office every day before lunch." He was quiet for a second as Charles and I exchanged glances. Then he did the unthinkable, and stated, "It's a good thing that you and Dad always tell me never to give up. I will make friends; it will be all right."

At that moment I became the student. My son had used my own words to jump-start me into acting like the professional I was prior to being a stay-at-home mom. Part of the problem was how I saw myself since reentering the workforce. So many of those I had interviewed with had dismissed me because I had opted to become a stay-at-home mother. Their opinions of my abilities had somehow become mine. It took a reality check for me to realize that being a stay-at-home mom is one of the most important jobs there is. I had not stopped working while I had been at home with my son; I had just changed my office location.

Armed with this truth, the following day at our weekly staff meeting, my staff met their *new* supervisor for the first time. If I could run a home, homeschool a child, and support another child who was in a year-round school, all while preparing meals, shopping, and keeping the house clean, I could most certainly run a unit. We discussed my policies for running the unit as well as my expectations for the staff, including a review of my expectations for calls to my home after 5:00 PM and on weekends when I was not on call. Any call that took me away from time with my family needed to constitute an emergency that would affect the health, safety, or welfare of those in our care.

The tides of change started that day and continued over the next year and a half. I did what I knew how to do best: listen, set limits, and empower others. Being a social worker is about effecting change in a positive manner that would otherwise not occur without some kind of outside influence. My staff and I learned to respect one another, and we learned how to work together as a team. When I resigned after two years to accept a job with the State Survey Agency, a party was held in my honor. My supervisor remarked, "I've never seen an entire building come together in such a positive manner to say good-bye to someone who has only been here a few years." Amid tears and well wishes, I had the opportunity to watch my staff, who had all grown so much, express their thoughts.

As I sat in my new office days later, the telephone rang. I had to suppress a smile at the familiar voice. My old staff exclaimed, "I told the new supervisor that she could not do that, because that is not how you did things!"

Bernetta Thorne-Williams

Beware the "I'ds" of March

"Stop it!" The words were said without a sideways glance, but with eyebrows raised in warning at the small hand that reached over to my laptop. "Mommy needs to finish this, honey."

The little hand withdrew, picked up the crayon, and continued to draw. "We gonna build a snowman today, Mommy?" Unable to keep the hope from bubbling up in his little-boy heart, he glanced to the window; the snowflakes had been falling, thick as fog since morning.

"Yeah, draw me a snowman, baby," I said, and squinted at the screen in front of me. "I'd better finish this before supper."

"But I'd rather make one with you, Mommy." He laid his little towhead onto his arm with resignation and began to color the carrot nose on his most perfect snowman.

My hands hovered over the keyboard. I no longer saw the spreadsheet on the computer screen. "I'd rather." Those words. "I'd rather." What was it about those words?

The first day I held the sweetness of my newborn child, cradled him, I felt at once the mixture of utter surrender and the fierce mother bear rise up in my heart. I spent days just smelling behind his ears, watching the soft brush of his eyelashes as they lay splayed upon his cheek, watching his fingers wrap around mine. What had I gotten myself into? How could I keep this perfect sweetness? How could I feel so in love and so fierce at the same time?

I asked these questions in a rhetorical, breathy way, not expecting Nana to really have the answers.

"Beware of the I'ds," she said so simply, winking slightly and smiling.

"The Ides? Like, of March?" I said, laughing, wondering just what new medication Nana was on, and how it was obviously affecting her brain.

She shook her head and brushed her hand across the soft forehead of the sleeping baby. "The I'ds."

"Not now, honey, I'd better finish the laundry."

"In a minute, baby, I'd better check on the roast."

"As soon as I'm done, I'd better finish this before dinner."

"The I'ds will rob you, sneak in and steal you minute by minute from the sticky fingers of love. They will distract you from the peanut butter kisses and ketchup hugs. The I'ds will tell you that the important things are the duties that must be done this minute, tasks that can't be put off. And suddenly you won't have their laundry to do; the roast dinner will be just for two—no longer accompanied by spilled milk and second helpings. The I'ds will make you forget that summer days do end, and that unmade snowmen melt away. So just beware of the I'ds, my child."

The little towhead boy did not look up as I softly closed the laptop. He giggled slightly as I smelled behind his little-boy ears. And he leapt up from the table when I said, "Let's go build a snowman, sweetie."

Heather Cook

Engraved on the Pages of Life

My youngest child was entering school. It was time for me to branch out. I felt I needed to be more than Bill's wife and the mother of our four children. It was time for me to find a job.

I was at a point in my life that I needed to contribute to the expansion of myself, to the family income, and perhaps to the future of the next generation, beyond my own children.

I would find a job from which I could be home when my kids were home from school. I wanted to work, but not jeopardize my family's happiness. I could do it, I was sure.

Like any woman on a mission, I took a brush-up course in typing, then applied for and became a library clerk in the grade school system.

Books! I would be carding, checking, labeling, shelving, reading, and stacking books. My job would be to help children select and check out their selections. I would be in charge of bulletin board displays, enticing youngsters to read books their teachers deemed enjoyable, entertaining, and educational.

Reading selections to the youngsters as their classes took turns in the library would be another responsibility I knew I would enjoy. I would help educate the students while they were in my charge by putting them in contact with the printed pages. I was to help expand their minds.

Those would be my duties.

"Your job category also includes lunchroom duty," I was told.

"Lunchroom duty?" There was not one book in the lunchroom, not one!

I soon learned there was more to the job than checking out books and stopping food fights in the cafeteria.

There was the child who always hung out at my desk, the kind of child who needed to know that you knew he or she was there.

I often wondered and worried about some of the children's needs. Some seemed to require more attention than the average child. What were they lacking in their home lives? Was there any way I could provide what they needed?

There was the child who hunkered in the corner and tried to disappear, not speaking unless spoken to, and then only the words that were necessary. *What issues is he facing in his life?* I wondered. Was there any way I could help him escape from his shell?

There was the boy who talked loudly, continually disrupting the class. It must be the only way he could attract attention, I surmised. I wondered why. How could I help him quiet down without snuffing out his spirit?

I'll never forget the little children who, I was sure, came to school without bathing, day after day. My heart ached for their needs. What must their circumstances be? That and other questions traveled home with me every night.

When I bathed my own children before putting them to bed, I couldn't help but think about the needs that must be in other homes in our community. How could I help fill the void in other children's lives created by neglect without stepping on their pride, their self-esteem, and embarrassing them?

Then there was the emotionally disturbed class that descended on me for their time in the library. They were sometimes accompanied by their teacher, and other times not.

Many of these children had difficulty with self-control. And it was not always easy for me to control them. I often found myself thinking about them and their problems, long after suppertime, when I talked with my secure children about their day at school.

There were so many children with so many problems. I did not have the knowledge to allow me to delve into their minds. Only my heart qualified me, and it, too, seemed inadequate as I embraced all that my eyes observed.

There was the youngster who was large in his build, lost somewhere in his mind; it was impossible to reach him, though I tried. *What mysteries lay hidden inside?* I wondered. Would he ever be able to escape? When I reached out to help, he seemed only to withdraw all the more. I, too, grew lost trying to find him as he hid behind the mask he wore.

There was the little boy who was mischievous, always in trouble, but everyone liked him. I talked to him, trying to encourage the wonderful lighthearted side he possessed. My reward was his smile. He, too, touched a special place in my heart. But I worried about him. Would he rise above the place in which he found himself? Would this little African American boy get past the race issue he so often faced? I knew he'd always be confronted with those who could not see the fact that hearts do not possess the color spectrum. God made hearts all the same color.

After a year and a half, I was diagnosed with multiple sclerosis and reluctantly gave up my job. That was more than thirty years ago.

I will never forget the privilege I had working with children. I was honored and blessed, and I hope I made a difference in some child's life, including my own children, during the time I spent in the school library.

In the years that have passed, I have occasionally met some of those former pupils.

"Hi, Mrs. King," they say, with a note of recognition. Yes, some do remember me.

While I worked in the school system, I handled many books. I don't remember many of their titles, but each child is forever engraved on my heart and my mind.

I believe it was I who was taught during the time I worked in the school library. Among other things, I learned how much my children needed a good mom, whether I worked outside the home or not. I also learned how some children have stay-at-home-mothers throughout their lives and still do not receive the love they need. Some things I learned broke my heart.

I learned how important every parent is in the life of his or her child; my children and I were all better off for my having worked outside the home, if even for a short time. We all appreciated one another more when I returned, having viewed life from a different perspective.

Knowledge and wisdom are often not found in books, but are engraved on the pages of life.

Betty King

Storm Day

It was 5:30 AM, and the annoying beep of the alarm clock woke me abruptly. There wasn't a minute to spare in the mornings; I had to report for work by 6:45 AM. The house was cold, and when I peeked through the window, what I saw made me want to scream! A heavy snow had fallen overnight, my husband was away, and my two student offspring were still sleeping. I turned on the radio just in time to hear the announcement of school closures. Yes, it was a "storm day," and the mere words turned me into a mass of anticipatory stress. What would these two partners in crime do, or undo, today?

My son was in twelfth grade, tall and strong, his sister in ninth grade, shorter but an equal accomplice with her brother in his many pranks and practical jokes. It was ten days before Christmas and, as any working mom knows, a time of enormous stress, too many demands, and constant fatigue. I had all the symptoms of the overworked, distressed working mom and more! "Storm days" were days when I wished the earth would swallow me whole! I well recalled the last free day these two had at home together. I came home to find my son with red marks all over his face and my daughter looking like she had swallowed the goldfish.

"What happened to you?" I asked my lanky son.

"She gave me the German claw when we were wrestling!" he reluctantly admitted.

So before leaving for work on that snowy morning, I told them about the storm day. Maybe they would sleep all day, or at least longer than usual. A mother can dream.

As my workday progressed, I received only two phone calls from home, so the situation there seemed under control in spite of my fears. Surely they would not repaint the house or scorch their feet on the burner of the stove, which had happened the day my son had tried to walk completely around the house without touching the floor! He was quite proud of that accomplishment!

Pushing those thoughts aside, I worked until 4:00 PM, then I left to start my never-ending list of errands. I finally arrived home, filled with dread, knowing that in eleven hours my two delinquents could have turned the world upside down, wounded each other, or reorganized the whole house. There was nothing they would not try or do! That was "a given," as the saying goes!

I was exhausted and a tad ill-tempered by the time I arrived home. The outside Christmas lights were on, and I entered our house to find the kitchen in a state of cleanliness and filled with the aroma of baked chicken. The reflections of the lights through the large window, combined with an immaculate house, the smell of supper cooking, and two young people with bigger smiles than I thought imaginable warmed my heart. They were so proud of their achievements.

"Well, since supper is underway, we'll have time to get the tree up tonight," I sputtered, still in a state of mild shock.

"Yeah, we'll help, Mom," they both answered. "Dad called, too."

He had told them when he would be home, and they

suggested that we should put up the tree in the recreation room so he would be surprised. Something was starting to make my skin itch, and I began to feel mild dizziness. *Is this really happening to me?* I wondered.

After the meal, they offered to do the dishes. This is surrealistic! I began watching the news, but the two cherubic beings stood in front of me and asked, "Aren't we going to do the tree?" Oh, yes, the tree.

The three of us headed to the family room where we always placed our tree. The smell of a fir tree met me as I opened the door. I turned on the light switch and suddenly the corner of the room lit up the most beautifully decorated Christmas tree! Gifts were underneath, and it looked simply glorious. Then the music of *Phil Coulter's Christmas* began to play. All I could do was stare. My eyes filled with tears, and I started to cry. It was the most amazing Christmas moment I had experienced in years.

I looked into the faces of the two young people who had been responsible for this gift, a gift I knew I would forever remember. Then I realized they were gifts to me, gifts I sometimes took for granted.

My love for them and my lifted spirits gave me a release from the fatigue I had been experiencing. The blush on their cheeks, combined with their looks of pride and achievement, was a moment engraved on my heart. I will never forget it, nor will they ever know how great a gift they had given me. How could I have underestimated them to such a degree?

In their thirties now, I mention it every Christmas. I hear the same thing every year. "Aw, Mom!" they say. "Everyone has heard that before!" I still think they are delightfully overjoyed at what they did for their mom that Christmas.

Whether I am with them or they are far away, I can see their bright eyes, feel my son's strong arms around my shoulders and my arms around my daughter's waist, hear the music, and see the most stunning Christmas tree glowing and decorated beautifully. They gave me the best Christmas gift of all. They gave of themselves and showed they understood and knew how their mom was feeling on that long-ago storm day.

Bonnie Jarvis-Lowe

More Chicken Soup?

Many of the stories and poems you have read in this book were submitted by readers like you who had read earlier Chicken Soup for the Soul books. We publish many Chicken Soup for the Soul books every year. We invite you to contribute a story to one of these future volumes.

Stories may be up to twelve hundred words and must uplift or inspire. You may submit an original piece, something you have read, or your favorite quotation on your refrigerator door.

To obtain a copy of our submission guidelines and a listing of upcoming Chicken Soup books, please write, fax, or check our website.

Please send your submissions to:

Chicken Soup for the Soul
Website: www.chickensoup.com
P.O. Box 30880
Santa Barbara, CA 93130
Fax: 805-563-2945

We will be sure that both you and the author are credited for your submission.

For information about speaking engagements, other books, audiotapes, workshops, and training programs, please contact any of our authors directly.

Supporting Others

The coauthors of *Chicken Soup for the Working Mom's Soul* have selected the Boys & Girls Club of Santa Barbara, Inc. to receive a portion of the book's proceeds.

The Boys & Girls Club of Santa Barbara, Inc. has been changing lives for nearly seventy years. Since 1938 when the first local club was opened, we have provided young people with hope and opportunity; a safe place to learn and grow; ongoing relationships with caring, adult professionals; and life-enhancing programs and character development experiences.

Located in the downtown region of Santa Barbara, the Boys & Girls Club of Santa Barbara fulfills an unquestionable need: keeping local children off the street, out of trouble, and in a positive learning environment. Most members live at or below the poverty level, while many are from broken homes, have a parent in jail, or are exposed to drug and alcohol abuse regularly. The best defense for these at-risk children is to remain actively engaged in programs that create a safe, enjoyable environment while providing cooperative, character-building activities.

When the last bell rings, thousands of Santa Barbara–area children will leave their classrooms around 3 PM. Some will go home to a parent, some will go to an extracurricular program, and some will go to work. However, many will go it alone. Lacking adult supervision or access to an after-school program, these young people will be in danger. We know from numerous studies and statistics that the rate of juvenile-related crime actually doubles during the hours after school. Studies show that from 3 PM to 4 PM, children are more likely to be involved in substance abuse, sexual activities, and crime.

It is crystal clear that all children are at risk in the after-school hours if left unsupervised—a problem that transcends demographics. That's why now, more then ever, we need the Boys & Girls Club. Every day across America, another 300 kids will join the club. That's 300 kids who will pick up a membership card instead of a gun or a needle or a knife.

Not only is the club a safe place for young people to gather after school, we also provide tested, proven, and nationally recognized programs that provide young people with the knowledge, skills, and attributes they need to pursue their dreams and succeed in life. These programs fall into five main categories: Character & Leadership Development; Education & Career Development; Health & Life Skills; The Arts; and Sports, Fitness & Recreation.

Today, the Boys & Girls Club of Santa Barbara serves more than 1,000 local youth and their families. Our club is staffed by paid, trained youth-development professionals, who, through a system of informal guidance, form strong bonds with young people and help them make smart choices in life. For many club members, club staff are the most influential positive adult role model in their lives.

There are still thousands of kids who need our help. Support a program that works—The Boys & Girls Club of Santa Barbara, the Positive Place for Kids.

For more information, please visit www.boysgirls.org or call 805-962-2382.

Who Is Jack Canfield?

Jack Canfield is the cocreator and editor of the Chicken Soup for the Soul series, which *Time* magazine has called "the publishing phenomenon of the decade." The series now has 105 titles with over 100 million copies in print in forty-one languages. Jack is also the co-author of eight other bestselling books, including *The Success Principles: How to Get from Where You Are to Where You Want to Be; Dare to Win; The Aladdin Factor; You've Got to Read This Book;* and *The Power of Focus: How to Hit Your Business and Personal and Financial Targets with Absolute Certainty.*

Jack has recently developed a telephone coaching program and an online coaching program based on his most recent book, *The Success Principles.* He also offers a seven-day Breakthrough to Success seminar every summer, which attracts 400 people from fifteen countries around the world.

Jack has conducted intensive personal and professional development seminars on the principles of success for over 900,000 people in twenty-one countries around the world. He has spoken to hundreds of thousands of others at numerous conferences and conventions and has been seen by millions of viewers on national television shows such as *The Today Show, Fox and Friends, Inside Edition, Hard Copy,* CNN's *Talk Back Live, 20/20, Eye to Eye,* the NBC *Nightly News,* and the CBS *Evening News.*

Jack is the recipient of many awards and honors, including three honorary doctorates and a Guinness World Records Certificate for having seven books from the Chicken Soup for the Soul series appearing on the *New York Times* bestseller list on May 24, 1998.

To write to Jack or for inquiries about Jack as a speaker, his coaching programs, or his seminars, use the following contact information:

The Canfield Companies
P.O. Box 30880 • Santa Barbara, CA 93130
Phone: 805-563-2935 • Fax: 805-563-2945
E-mail: info@jackcanfield.com
Website: www.jackcanfield.com

Who Is Mark Victor Hansen?

In the area of human potential, no one is more respected than Mark Victor Hansen. For more than thirty years, Mark has focused solely on helping people from all walks of life reshape their personal vision of what's possible. His powerful messages of possibility, opportunity, and action have created powerful change in thousands of organizations and millions of individuals worldwide.

He is a sought-after keynote speaker, bestselling author, and marketing maven. Mark's credentials include a lifetime of entrepreneurial success and an extensive academic background. He is a prolific writer with many bestselling books, such as *The One-Minute Millionaire*, *Cracking the Millionaire Code*, *How to Make the Rest of Your Life the Best of Your Life*, *The Power of Focus*, *The Aladdin Factor*, and *Dare to Win*, in addition to the Chicken Soup for the Soul series. Mark has made a profound influence through his library of audios, videos, and articles in the areas of big thinking, sales achievement, wealth building, publishing success, and personal and professional development.

Mark is the founder of the MEGA Seminar Series. MEGA Book Marketing University and Building Your MEGA Speaking Empire are annual conferences where Mark coaches and teaches new and aspiring authors, speakers, and experts on building lucrative publishing and speaking careers. Other MEGA events include MEGA Info-Marketing and My MEGA Life.

As a philanthropist and humanitarian, Mark works tirelessly for organizations such as Habitat for Humanity, American Red Cross, March of Dimes, Childhelp USA, and many others. He is the recipient of numerous awards that honor his entrepreneurial spirit, philanthropic heart, and business acumen. He is a lifetime member of the Horatio Alger Association of Distinguished Americans, an organization that honored Mark with the prestigious Horatio Alger Award for his extraordinary life achievements.

Mark Victor Hansen is an enthusiastic crusader of what's possible and is driven to make the world a better place.

Mark Victor Hansen & Associates, Inc.
P.O. Box 7665 • Newport Beach, CA 92658
Phone: 949-764-2640 • Fax: 949-722-6912
Website: www.markvictorhansen.com

Who Is Patty Aubery?

As the president of Chicken Soup for the Soul Enterprises and a #1 *New York Times* bestselling coauthor, Patty Aubery knows what it's like to juggle work, family, and social obligations—along with the responsibility of developing and marketing the more than 80 million *Chicken Soup* books and licensed goods worldwide.

She knows because she's been with Jack Canfield's organization since the early days—before Chicken Soup took the country by storm. Jack was still telling these heartwarming stories then, in his training programs, workshops, and keynote presentations, and it was Patty who directed the labor of love that went into compiling and editing the original 101 Chicken Soup stories. Later, she supported the daunting marketing effort and steadfast optimism required to bring it to millions of readers worldwide.

Today, Patty is the mother of two active boys—J. T. and Chandler—exemplifying that special combination of commitment, organization, and life balance all working women want to have. She's been known to finish at the gym by 6:00 AM, guest-host a radio show at 6:30, catch a flight by 9:00 to close a deal—and be back in time for soccer with the kids. But perhaps the most notable accolade for this special working woman is the admiration and love her friends, family, staff, and peers hold for her.

Of her part in the Chicken Soup family, Patty says, "I'm always encouraged, amazed, and humbled by the storytellers I meet when working on any Chicken Soup book, but by far the most poignant have been those stories of women in the working world, overcoming incredible odds and—in the face of all challenges—excelling as only women could do."

Patty is also the coauthor of several other bestselling titles: *Chicken Soup for the Christian Soul, Christian Family Soul,* and *Christian Woman's Soul, Chicken Soup for the Expectant Mother's Soul, Chicken Soup for the Sister's Soul,* and *Chicken Soup for the Surviving Soul.*

She is married to a successful international entrepreneur, Jeff Aubery, and together with J. T. and Chandler they make their home in Santa Barbara, California. Patty can be reached at:

Self-Esteem Seminars
P.O. Box 30880
Santa Barbara, CA 93130
Phone: 805-563-2935
Fax: 805-563-2945

Contributors

Margaret Haefner Berg is an associate professor of music education at the University of Colorado and the mother of two boys. In her spare time she enjoys hiking and playing the violin. She can be reached at margaret.berg @colorado.edu.

Peggy Bert is a graduate of Upper CLASS Speakers, a certified Personality Plus Trainer, a private pilot, and holds an M.A. in theological studies. A sought-after speaker for conferences and retreats, Peggy specializes in teaching personal growth topics, communication skills, and relationship enrichment. She is completing her first book. Publishing credits include.*Chicken Soup for the Soul* and *Marriage Partnership* magazine. Her family enjoys skiing, beach walking, and traveling. To find out more about Peggy, visit www.PeggyBert.com.

Stephanie Ray Brown of Henderson, Kentucky, is a part-time reading instructor and a full-time mother to Savannah and Cameron. She salutes all working mothers, especially those who are single. She dedicates this story to her favorite single mother, Rita Ray, who worked as a factory worker, cashier, coal miner, and nurse so she could send all three of her children to college, as well as herself.

Vanessa Ann Cain married her high school sweetheart and is currently living in West Tennessee. In addition to humorous stories about her children, she pens poetry, children's book manuscripts, and newspaper articles for the *State Gazette* in Dyersburg, where she works as a reporter. She can be reached at van3669@msn.com.

Debi Callies is the author of *Stay Strong, Stay Safe, My Son,* a book describing her challenges in sending her son Robert to war. Debi is also the proud mother of three other children: Demi, Kaila, and Drew. She teaches at Ottawa University in Phoenix, Arizona. She can be reached at vpmm@cox.net, or visit www.marinemom.info.

Stephanie Chandler is a small business expert and author of *From Entrepreneur to Infopreneur: Make Money with Books, E-Books, and Information Products* (John Wiley & Sons, December 2006). She is also the founder of www.BusinessInfo Guide.com, a directory of resources for entrepreneurs, and www.Pro PublishingServices.com, a custom writing business that specializes in electronic newsletters.

Dorothy Megan Clifton is seventy years old, so it's not easy being brief about her life experiences. She is active in community theater and loves playing the piano. Dorothy is also an avid reader and active within her church. She's been blessed with two great kids and five grandchildren. Life is good.

Karen Cogan enjoys writing stories for both children and adults. She has several books available in library collections. When she is not writing, she enjoys time with her family and playing with her dogs. To find out more about Karen, please visit karencogan.com.

Heather Cook is a writer and mother. She lives in Calgary, Alberta, with her husband and two children. Heather enjoys reading, horseback riding, and an elusive thing called peace and quiet. Her book, *Rookie Reiner,* is due in 2008 from Trafalgar Square Books.

Susan Courtad knows a thing or two about Hershey's chocolate and juggling many roles. A full-time working mom, she recently completed her first novel about a single mother learning to balance parenting, dating, and working in corporate America. She can be reached at susanwrites@zoominternet.net.

Diane M. Covington graduated with honors from UCLA and became a successful entrepreneur and then an award-winning journalist. Her writing has appeared in national magazines, newspapers, and on NPR. She divides her time between her apple farm in Northern California and the beaches of Southern California. She can be reached at www.dianecovington.com.

Margaret P. Cunningham lives with her husband, Tom, on Alabama's beautiful gulf coast, where she enjoys reading, writing, family, and friends. Her stories have appeared in magazines and anthologies, including four previous Chicken Soup for the Soul books. She has just finished her first novel, entitled *Lily's Garden.* She can be reached at peggymob@aol.com.

Crystal Davis received her master's degree in psychiatric social work, with honors, from Wayne State University in Detroit. She is the author of a newly released self-help book, *A Journey to Wholeness: Looking For Love in All the Wrong Places.* She is a school social worker with the Detroit Public Schools and has been providing services to students for fourteen years. You can email her at cmdavid628@sbcglobal.net.

Jane Elsdon is an award-winning author of fiction, nonfiction, and poetry. She is a past poet laureate of San Luis Obispo, California. She has published over two hundred poems and short stories. The joys of her life are her husband, family, friends, and her art. She lives in Atascadero, California.

Maya Fleischmann is a writer, wife, and mother of three. Raised in Hong Kong and the United States, she currently resides in Vietnam, where she continues to write and teach. She is an avid traveler, book lover, and advocate for literacy and education. She can be reached at zenpoole@yahoo.com.

Dorothy K. Fletcher has taught high school English for thirty-five years. She won first place in the 2006 Robert Frost Poetry Contest and was invited to speak at the Library of Congress in December 2006. She loves writing and has published three books. To find out more about Dorothy, please visit www.dorothykfletcher.com.

Peggy Frezon is a freelance writer from New York. Her publishing credits include *Guideposts, Sweet 16, Positive Thinking, Angels on Earth, Teaching Tolerance, Chicken Soup for the Soul, Soul Matters,* and more. She enjoys spending time with her husband, Mike, and kids, Kate and Andy. For more information about Peggy, please visit http://peggyfrezon.googlepages.com.

Sally Friedman is a mommy-writer. Her family has been at the center of her life—and work—for decades because of her passion for personal essays. Another generation—her seven grandchildren—now provides additional inspiration. She can be reached at pinegander@aol.com.

Tony Gilbert, a native of southwest Georgia, is a graduate of the University of Southern Mississippi and the University of Georgia. A former teacher, coach, and marathon runner, Tony was a sportswriter for many years and has authored three books.

Christina Guzman lives in San Jose, California, with her three children, Karinah, Alexis, and Justice. She is a full-time single working mom. She enjoys spending time with her family and writing poetry. She can be reached at christinapguzman@yahoo.com.

Pamela Hackett Hobson, a busy mother of Tom and Mike, is the author of *The Bronxville Book Club* and *The Silent Auction.* Pam's work was featured in the *New York Times* article "Buzzzz, Murmurs Follow Novel." To find out more about Pam and her novels, please visit www.pamelahobson.com.

Linda Hanson has worked as a respiratory therapist at eight hospitals in four states over the past thirty years. She is happily married and the proud mother of two grown children, who are both now terrific cooks.

Jonny Hawkins draws cartoons full time from his home in Sherwood, Michigan, alongside his lovely wife, Carissa, the CFO of his tiny humor enterprise. They are parents to two young boys, Nate and Zach, and their brand-new baby, Kara, born January 1, 2007. Jonny dedicates the cartoons in this book to Carissa and his little redhead, Kara Elise.

Miriam Hill is coauthor of *Fabulous Florida* and a frequent contributor to Chicken Soup for the Soul books. Her publishing credits include *The Christian Science Monitor, Grit, St. Petersburg Times,* and Poynter Online. Miriam's manuscript received Honorable Mention for Inspirational Writing in the 75th Annual *Writer's Digest* Writing Competition.

Jo Ann Holbrook freelance writes from her rural southern Indiana home, shared with husband, Gil, and their horses, dogs, cats, and chickens. Her weekly newspaper column, "Heartbeats & Hoofprints," is often about animals and the people they own. She travels and is keen on horseback riding and life. She can be reached at gradejo@aol.com.

Melanie Howard is an award-winning writer whose work has appeared in *SELF, Glamour, Baby Talk,* and other national publications. She lives in Virginia with her husband, two children, and dog. Melanie enjoys travel, tennis, and family time, and goes to great lengths to avoid doing laundry. She can be reached at MHoward57@aol.com.

Bonnie Jarvis-Lowe is a registered nurse from Newfoundland, Canada. Her nursing career, family, photography, and writing have been her lifelong passions. She has two grown children and a granddaughter. Now retired, she has more time to devote to her writing and photography and family, and her much loved boating.

Lynda Johnson received undergraduate and graduate degrees in chemistry from the University of Cincinnati in Ohio. She is a wife and mother to the most wonderful family in the world. Hobbies include lampwork glass, jewelry, cooking, and gardening. By day, she works in quality assurance for a major pharmaceutical company.

"Prayer cheerleader for the Lord" is how **Eva Juliuson** describes herself. She encourages others to delve deeper into a prayer relationship with God. She offers an e-mail ministry that sends out regular short prayers to jump start others' personal prayer life. If you are interested in receiving her e-mails, contact her at evajuliuson@hotmail.com.

Kimberly Kimmel, a journalist, songwriter, former editor for a music/fashion magazine, and writing instructor, has sold numerous articles and short stories. She has interviewed dozens of celebrities, mostly for the teen market. Kimberly has two grown children and calls Los Angeles home. She can be reached at kimberlybkimmel@hotmail.com.

Betty King is the author of *It Takes Two Mountains to Make a Valley; But—It Was in the Valleys I Grew; The Fragrance of Life;* and *Safe and Secure in the Palm of His Hand.* She is a columnist of two weekly newspaper columns. She lives with the disease MS.

Mimi Greenwood Knight is a freelance writer living in Folsom, Louisiana, with her husband, David, and their four children, Haley, Molly, Hewson, and Jonah, plus four dogs, four cats, and one chuckleheaded bird. She enjoys Bible study, butterfly gardening, baking, and the lost art of letter writing. She can be reached at djknight@airmail.net.

Margaret Lang is a freelance writer with twenty-six published stories. As a speaker/teacher in the United States and overseas, she teaches women about their value and teens about purity and purpose. Her greatest joy is coming home to her two young granddaughters. You can contact her at margielang @yahoo.com.

Pat Winters Lauro is a freelance journalist whose work frequently appears in *The New York Times*. She has a BA from Fordham University and a master's degree from Columbia University. The mother of three children, she lives with her husband in New Jersey where she works full time as a professor of English and journalism. She is currently working on a chic-lit novel.

Mary Dixon Lebeau is an employment counselor and freelance writer. She and her husband, Scott, live in New Jersey, where they sneak a peek at "real summers" through the eyes of their five children. Mary has written for *Family Circle, Parenting, Parents,* and three previous editions of Chicken Soup for the Soul. She can be reached at marylebeau@comcast.net.

Sheryl McCormick is a proud single parent of seven-year-old Dylan. She was a medical technician in the Canadian Forces. She has since been discharged from the military to be able to spend more time with her son. Dylan is her inspiration for this story. Sheryl aspires to be published in the children's market.

Sharon McElroy is published in *Chicken Soup for the Sister's Soul 2* and award-winner of the annual publisher's award for Artist Profile Press, Inc., for a poem on the subject of writing. Additionally, Sharon was awarded the Notable American Woman Award for respectfully reflecting leadership and positively inspiring the spirit of people worldwide through her inspirational poetry. Please feel free to e-mail Sharon at sharonmcelroy@hotmail.com.

Dahlynn McKowen is the dedicated mother of two and a full-time author. She is an active coauthor for Chicken Soup for the Soul books and has created many titles, including *Fisherman's Soul, Entrepreneur's Soul, Soul in Menopause, Sisters' and Brothers' Soul,* and the upcoming *Female Entrepreneur's Soul.* To find out more about Dahlynn, please visit www.PublishingSyndicate.com.

You're danged if you do and danged if you don't, so you might just as well follow the dirt road in your soul to **Carol Mell**'s "Humbug Mountain" at NewWest.net and the *Albuquerque Journal* North Edition, where she takes a humorous gander at Taos, New Mexico, and all places west. She can be reached at carolmell@msn.com.

Pat Moore, a professional organizer and speaker since 1991, was a national household tips columnist for six years and one of the first organizers to appear on HGTV. Her parenting priorities created a wonderful new business of organizing photos and creating customized scrapbooks for clients nationwide. She can be reached at patsmoore@verizon.net.

Maryjo Faith Morgan belongs to Colorado Authors' League (www.coloradoauthors.org) and hosts a Weekly Writers' Workshop, which furthers members' writing careers. She produces a wide variety of written work, including business text, magazine features, and creative nonfiction. Her husband, Fred (www.fredsusedwebsites.com), is the Webmaster behind www.maryjofaithmorgan.com. They also enjoy tandem biking together.

Cynthia Morningstar received her bachelor of music in piano performance from Ouachita Baptist University in Arkansas in 1979. She is a pastor's wife at Sandusky Presbyterian Church in Sandusky, Michigan, where she also works as a librarian, piano teacher, and choir and handbell director.

Jan Morrill has written several short stories and memoir essays and is currently working on a novel. She graduated with honors with a bachelor of arts degree from Langston University. Jan lives in Fayetteville, Arkansas, with her husband, and enjoys sailing and traveling. She can be reached at janmorrill @sbcglobal.net.

Ann Morrow and her family live in Custer, South Dakota, where she writes humorous/inspirational pieces. Her columns and short stories have appeared in a variety of publications, including previous Chicken Soup for the Soul books. She can be reached at nova@gwtc.net.

Jennifer Nicholson works in a quality assurance role with a leading worldwide pharmaceutical company. She is also a wife and mother of two beautiful children. In her spare time, she loves to scrapbook, watch her kids' soccer and hockey games, and write.

Linda O'Connell has been an early childhood educator for thirty years. She is a multigenre freelance writer and writing teacher. She has been published in many anthologies, literary magazines, and newspapers. She enjoys camping with her husband and treasures the time she spends with their grandchildren. She can be reached at Billin7@juno.com.

Jennifer Oliver, author of *Four Ears: Works of Heart*, owes her inspiration to househubby, Stephen, and to their magnificent creative life forces: Cody, Ethan, Matthew, and Madison. Her stories have appeared in several Chicken Soup books and other heartwarming publications.

Tiffany O'Neill was raised in California's Central Valley. She now makes her home in New Jersey, where she enjoys life as a freelance writer, wife, and stay-at-home mom of two daughters. She can be reached at oneill_tiffany@yahoo.com.

Erica Orloff is the author of *Spanish Disco, Mafia Chic, Double Down,* and other novels about glamorous women, none of whom bear much resemblance to her real, messy, but joy-filled life. She lives with her family and assorted disobedient pets in Virginia. To find out more about Erica, please visit www.ericaorloff.com.

Joan Paquette is a freelance and children's writer who lives outside of Boston, Massachusetts. She is still juggling work and motherhood, and loving every minute of it.

Mark Parisi's "Off the Mark" comic, syndicated since 1987, is distributed by United Media. Mark's humor also graces greeting cards, T-shirts, calendars, magazines, newsletters, and books. Lynn is his wife and business partner.

Their daughter, Jen, contributes with inspiration (as do three cats). To find out more about Mark, please visit www.offthemark.com.

Kathleen Partak has been writing a weekly e-mail column for the past seven years called the Monday Motivator. Kathleen has done several short-term columns on telephony, today's technology, and mortgages. She is the proud wife of an Army soldier and mother of three-year-old Mason. She also has several children's books and a motivational book in the works. She can be reached at Kdpartak@yahoo.com.

Stephen A. Peterson received his bachelor of arts and master of science degrees from Indiana University–Bloomington, his doctor of philosophy from the University of Oklahoma, and is persuing his doctor of philosophy in counseling psychology at Oklahoma State University. Stephen has written more than 500 stories and scholarly articles and more than thirty books in the areas of military history, psychology, and anthropology. He is a recent military retiree and plans more books in the near future. He can be reached at indianpete2@aol.com.

Stephanie Piro lives in New Hampshire with her husband, daughter, and three cats. She is one of King Features' team of women cartoonists "Six Chix" (she is the Saturday chick!). Her new book, *My Cat Loves Me Naked,* is available at bookstores everywhere. She also designs gift items for her company, Strip T's. To find out more about Stephanie, please visit www.stephaniepiro.com. She can be reached at 27 River Road, Farmington, NH 03835, or e-mail stephaniepiro@verizon.net.

Mindy Potts, wife and mother of two, earned her master's in education from the University at Albany in 1992. She works in elementary education and writes for a small paper with a big name, the *OK Times & Hudson River Sampler.* She also dabbles in writing children's literature. She can be reached at pottsteam@yahoo.com.

Felice Prager is a freelance writer from Scottsdale, Arizona, with credits in local, national, and international publications. She is a multisensory educational therapist and works with adults and children with moderate to severe learning disabilities. To find out more about Felice, please visit Write Funny! at www.writefunny.com.

After spending several years working in social services, **Britt Prince** returned to school to earn her master of arts in elementary teaching from George Fox University in 2007. She enjoys spending time with her family, traveling, collecting vintage toys, and writing stories. Britt can be reached at britterin73@yahoo.com.

Winter D. Prosapio is a Hill Country essayist and writer, and writes the weekly humor column "Crib Notes." Her writing has appeared in the *Christian Science Monitor, Texas Co-op Power* magazine, regional and local publications, Working Mothers and several online sites. To find out more about Winter, please visit winterdprosapio.com.

Emily Rider-Longmaid wrote "Moms Know Everything" at age thirteen. Now seventeen, Emily is a high school junior in Massachusetts. She plays soccer and basketball and is a member of her school's Community Service Board. She speaks Spanish and French, enjoys reading and writing, and loves spending time with family and friends.

Brenda Rosales Rincon is on a career hiatus to focus on motherhood and writing. As of press time, Brenda owns twenty pairs of black shoes and fifteen black skirts. She and her husband, both USC graduates, live in Southern California with their seven-year-old daughter, a Seinfeld fan with comedic aspirations of her own. She can be reached at brincon@dc.rr.com.

Bruce Robinson is an award-winning, internationally published cartoonist whose work has appeared in numerous consumer and trade periodicals, including the *National Enquirer, The Saturday Evening Post, Woman's World, The Sun, First, Highlights for Children,* and more. He is also author of the cartoon book *Good Medicine.* He can be reached at cartoonsbybrucerobinson@hotmail.com.

Dan Rosandich operates www.danscartoons.com, where over 3,000 cartoons are available for licensing at reasonable fees. Dan also specializes in "custom" cartoons, which can be used for any professional projects. Dan can be reached at dan@danscartoons.com.

Harriet May Savitz has over twenty-four books published by major publishers. Savitz's book *Run Don't Walk* was made into an *ABC Afterschool Special* produced by Henry Winkler. Recipient of the PSLA Outstanding Pennsylvania Author Award, Savitz now has her groundbreaking books about the disabled back in print. To find out more about Harriet, please visit www.harrietmaysavitz.com, or she can be reached at hmaysavitz@aol.com.

Deborah Shouse is a speaker, writer, and editor. Her writing has appeared in *Reader's Digest, Newsweek,* and *Spirituality & Health.* She is donating all proceeds from her book *Love in the Land of Dementia: Finding Hope in the Caregiver's Journey* to Alzheimer's programs and research. To find out more about Deborah, please visit www.thecreativityconnection.com.

Elizabeth Bussey Sowdal is a registered nurse and freelance writer living in Oklahoma City. She is married and has four quite remarkable children. Initially, she thought the children would provide her with a lot to write about, but she has grown to love them.

Judy Spence worked twenty-five years at Southwestern Bell Telephone Company before retiring in 1993, but she says her favorite job was parenting daughters Stephanie and Shelby, now grown. Judy enjoys reading, traveling, and playing with her sweet granddaughters Micah, age four, in Edmond, OK, and Avery, age three, in Albuquerque, NM.

Ken Swarner is author of *Whose Kids Are These Anyway?* He can be reached at kenswarner@aol.com.

Pamela Teague lives in Edmond, Oklahoma, where she works as a Realtor. She enjoys reading, writing poems and children's stories, cooking, ministering in her church, and spending time with friends and family. Pamela's publication credits include a short story, "Mattie's a Pipsqueak," published by *On the Line* magazine, and "Baby in the Mirror," published by the International Library of Poetry in their latest collection of poems, *Twilight Musings*.

Stephanie Welcher Thompson's four-year-old daughter, Micah, says, "Mom makes Chicken Soup in the office." Often the subject of stories, Micah doesn't seem to mind, yet. As founder of State of Change, Stephanie hosted a radio show and writes syndicated newspaper columns. She is a freelance writer. She can be reached at P.O. Box 1502, Edmond, OK 73083, or e-mail stephanie@stateofchange.net.

Bernetta Thorne-Williams was born and raised in Washington D.C. She received a BS and BA from NC Wesleyan College. Bernetta currently resides in North Carolina with her husband and two sons. She is a contributing author of two other Chicken Soup for the Soul books. Bernetta has completed several romance novels. E-mail her at BernettaThorneWilliams@yahoo.com.

Tanya Tyler is a writer and editor in the advertising creative services department of the *Herald-Leader* newspaper in Lexington, Kentucky. She is also an ordained minister in the Christian Church (Disciples of Christ). She can be reached at tanya.tyler@insightbb.com.

Arlene Uslander is the author of twelve nonfiction books, primarily in the field of child development, parenting, and humor, and has won several media awards for excellence in journalism. Uslander is now retired from full-time teaching, spends her time writing, editing, traveling with her husband, Ira, enjoying their grandchildren, Eric, Ryan, and Carly, and doing some substitute teaching—just to stay in touch with what's on kids' minds, and in their hearts, today.

Mary Vallo is a writer and editor of the regional parenting magazine *The Parent Paper*. She lives with her husband and three children in Pearl River, New York. She can be reached at maryvallo@optonline.net.

Shirley Warren describes her writing as the best excuse she can find for avoiding housework. Her works are based on her desire to find inspiration in ordinary day-to-day experiences. She resides in Massachusetts with her family, where they choose to live happily ever after. She can be reached at Shirley_Warren@mac.com.

Jo Webnar is an author and freelance writer currently living aboard a trawler that cruises the East Coast and Florida. Her first romance, *Twilight,* is offered as an e-book. *Savign Tampa* is a romantic suspense offered by her literary agent. She is working on her third novel, *Hidden Death,* which is set in the Florida Keys. For more information about Jo, please visit her website at www.jowebnar.com.

Jennifer L. White is self-employed as a media consultant in Massachusetts. She is married to Mark, with a son, Colin, and daughter, Devon. Jennifer and Colin have published a book of humor poetry and illustrations entitled *Coolhead Luke and Other Stories*. Look for it at www.amazon.com.

Nicole M. Whitney is the founder, producer, and host of *News for the Soul*, a popular radio show and home to the largest online, totally free, life-changing audio resource, found at www.newsforthesoul.com. By thinking differently, she has transcended the three "incurable" diseases mentioned in this story. To find out more about Nicole, please visit www.newsforthesoul.com.